"Lord have mercy—I needed *BETTER*. I needed Melvin's imagination, wisdom, commitment to grace, and the seriousness and playfulness with which he approaches God, scripture and love. The only way forward for people of light is to wake up to our faith as a unifying source of light and healing. In *BETTER,* Melvin shows us the way."

—Glennon Doyle Melton, author of *Love Warrior* and founder of Momastery.com and Together Rising

"Melvin Bray's *BETTER* deserves your time and attention. It will introduce you to the wisdom of one of the most delightful and insightful moral and spiritual educators I've ever met. It will help you read the Bible in a fresh and desperately needed way. And it will equip you to become a better teller of better stories to build a better world."

—Brian D. McLaren, author/activist

"A breath of fresh air for people suffocating under rigid, compassionless faith traditions that marginalize Grace, Justice, and Compassion. The world is in need of better stories, a better way, and a new lens to see an old story. In an age of fear, racial anxiety, and xenophobia we need this radical epistle of love more than ever to reroute the course of our beloved yet static institutions. Bravo! This is the book I have been praying for."

—Otis Moss III, Trinity United Church of Christ (Chicago), author of *Blue Note Preaching in a Post-Soul World*

"Bray positions *BETTER* as an escape route for persons living under religious oppression. He masterfully recalibrates the tension between faith and formation. He captures the cadence of culture and argues that knowing how to survive doesn't make us better. Bray has his finger on the pulse of the fate awaiting [faith] communities that refuse to re-imagine their story. *BETTER* is the sparkplug needed to ignite any beloved community to bend toward justice."

—K. Edwin Bryant, author of *Paul and the Rise of the Slave*

"For those frustrated by the way our faith stories have been held captive by fundamentalism and toxic religiosity, Melvin Bray calls us to compost rotting ideology into life-giving spirituality. His effective retelling of faith narratives moves us into *better* ways of living in Beloved Community. Read this book and be equipped, inspired, and challenged to go tell better stories in your community!"

—Cindy Wang Brandt, author of *Outside In: Ten Christian Voices We Can't Ignore,* Patheos blogger at *Unfundamentalist Parenting*

BETTER

WAKING UP TO WHO WE COULD BE

MELVIN BRAY

Foreword by Brittney Cooper

chalice
press

Saint Louis, Missouri

An imprint of Christian Board of Publication

Cover design: Bidemi (Bd) Oladele
Interior design: Connie Hui-Chu Wang

Scripture marked ESV is from *The Holy Bible, English Standard Version®* (ESV®), copyright © 2001 by Crossway, a publishing ministry of Good News Publishers. Used by permission. All rights reserved. Scripture marked NASB is taken from the *New American Standard Bible®*, Copyright © 1960, 1962, 1963, 1968, 1971, 1972, 1973, 1975, 1977, 1995 by The Lockman Foundation. Used by permission. (www.Lockman.org)

Scripture marked NIV is taken from the *Holy Bible, New International Version®*, NIV®. Copyright © 1973, 1978, 1984, 2011 by Biblica, Inc.TM Used by permission of Zondervan. All rights reserved worldwide. www.zondervan.com. The "NIV" and "New International Version" are trademarks registered in the United States Patent and Trademark Office by Biblica, Inc.TM

Scripture marked NRSV is from the *New Revised Standard Version of the Bible,* copyright 1989, Division of Christian Education of the National Council of the Churches of Christ in the United States of America. Used by permission. All rights reserved.

Cover art: Standing Rock photo by John Duffy, copyright ©2016. Used under authority of Creative Commons license, https://commons.wikimedia.org/wiki/File:NoDAPL-JohnDuffy.png. Emanuel 9 anniversary march photo, copyright © 2016 by John Fitzgerald Johnson. Used under Creative Commons license.

Photos on pages 10, 25, 74, 94, 95, 97, 114, 137, 140, and 142 are by **Nikole Lim.** Used with permission. All rights reserved. Photos on pages 28, 35, 50, 56, 104, 120, and 134 are by **Carlton Mackey**. Used with permission. All rights reserved. Photo on page 15 is by **Jim Lord** of the *Obama Hope Poster* by Shepard Fairey. Digital image. *Wikimedia Commons*. N.p., 4 Feb. 2008. https://commons.wikimedia.org/wiki/File:Obama_Hope_Poster_Shepard_Fairey.jpg. Illustration on page 27 is a **P. Graham Dunn** clock on Amazon.com in 2016. Historical illustrations on pages 45-47 are in the public domain and widely available online. Photo on page 83 is of Arch Goins and his family, donated to Wikicommons.org by Barbara Goins, public domain. On page 105, the cartoon entitled "A Concise History of Black-White Relations in the USA" is by **Barry Deutsch**, copyright ©2008 by Barry Deutsch. The other cartoon is by **Dana Simpson**, copyright ©2004 by Dana Simpson. Both cartoons used with permission. All rights reserved. Photo on page 115 is from **USAid Africa Bureau**, public domain. Photo on page 127 of Sitting Bull copyright ©1885 by **D.F. Barry**. Image available from the United States Library of Congress's Prints and Photographs division under the digital ID cph.3c11147. Illustration on page 169 is of the "Now Is Zen Wall Clock" available at cafepress.com.

ChalicePress.com

Print ISBN 9780827203082   EPUB ISBN 9780827203099   EPDF ISBN 9780827203105

Printed in the USA.

Contents

To my mom, who taught me to question.

To my dad, who taught me to tell stories.

To my wife, who tells me I can.

To my children, for whom I strive for BETTER.

I also dedicate this project to those like me who live with the restless intuition that BETTER is possible and labor to be a part of it. Also, to those who've been harmed by hostile faith stories.

Foreword

By Brittney Cooper

"This is my story." Those are the beginning words of the chorus to one of my favorite hymns, "Blessed Assurance." When we come together in collective worship to sing this song, Christians are supposed to walk away believing that our faith lies in our investment in a *singular* story. As a rule, Christians are supposed to be invested in telling the *same* story, the *same* way, every time. A little creativity is welcomed in the sermonic moment, but too much deviation gets folks' undies in a bunch. Words like "heresy" and "blasphemy" begin floating in the word clouds above the heads of people of faith, if anyone dares to try to tell the story anew.

How many of us have been hustled into the church equivalent of the principal's office or pulled to the side and scolded by a persnickety lady with a dog-eared Bible because we asked one too many questions in Sunday School or Bible Study? For so many of us, *this* is *our story*. Our story has been about giving up surety and certainty to find the blessing in our questions. What if the true foretaste of glory comes at the moment that we let go of everything we thought we knew? What if it comes when we ask the questions we have really been wanting to ask, but feared asking? It seemed to be that way for Sarah, mother of the skeptical, when she asked, "Shall I have pleasure?" It seemed to be that way for suffering Job, when he begged, "Why have you made me your target?" It was even that way for Jesus, when he finally gave in and asked, "My God, why have you left me here among these terrible people without any help?"

Surely that is a question that some of you have wanted to ask at one time or another. Surely you have asked God where your help was coming from. I know I have. And frankly, if one more person tells me, "the Bible is clear," they might get a tongue-lashing that would impress even the once rogue Apostle Peter.

Melvin Bray's *BETTER: Waking Up to Who We Could Be* has arrived to help us. He challenges us to imagine the stories—our personal stories, our collective stories, and our national stories—differently. Bray's book gives us the agency to come to the stories that have anchored us with fresh eyes and all the questions we have. Stories of faith and possibility are meant to free us, not to hold us hostage. We can hold onto our stories without letting our stories have a death grip on us.

Author Brian McLaren has written about how the Bible is a kind of library, a collection of stories that invite our engagement. Melvin Bray shows up here as the beloved, contrarian, radical librarian, who helps you move through the space finding all the great stories and hidden gems you never expected to see. *BETTER* offers fresh tools to help people of faith (or not of faith, for that matter) read and tell better the stories that shape us, first and foremost by reminding us, that our stories should always be in service of building beloved community and never about excluding people from it.

For a radical feminist, Southern, country, Black girl professor like me, the story has to be told differently in order for me to see myself in it, because our collective and national stories were intentionally told for so long to exclude people like me. But I can see myself in Bray's telling in chapter 2 the story of the Syrophoenician woman who trades barbs with Jesus because he had something she needed. I hear her snarky "boy bye," when Jesus tries to dismiss her. By being able to tell the story differently, in what Bray calls a COMPOSTable way, by opening up to the possibility that the women in Jesus's community challenged him and questioned him, a story of the faithful emerges that embraces and encourages the curious and skeptical ones among us. That's fresh air—good news—for women like me for sure!

Bray's book is unique, too, because it takes on topics that even progressive Christians handle in a clunky manner. In our communities of radical Jesus lovers, we have gotten progressively better at rejecting homophobia, embracing queer folks, and creating a theological discourse that acknowledges the import and value of LGBTQIA people in our communities. To be clear, there is no Christianity without queer folks, who have always been among us. In the Black Christian churches from which I come, we have always relied on the ministry and worship labor of people whose silence we demanded when it came to their intimate lives. Those are hard truths that progressive Christians of all stripes are getting better at telling.

But race is a different matter entirely. Sometimes I wonder if all the progressive Christians are white. This whiteness is overwhelming when I read the books of my faves, and those books deal well with questions of queer identity, gender politics, and the problem of poverty, while struggling to take on the question of racism. Bray doesn't let progressive Christianity off the hook on matters of race. He assumes that his Blackness has a place in the story, that acknowledging the myriad ways it shows up can make the stories of beloved community better. But he does intuitively understand something that really matters—that for so many who want our faith stories to be *better*, there isn't an absence of interest, but rather a lack of tools.

This book is chock-full of tools and models for reimagining that allow us to go back to our sacred stories and see them differently. Each chapter sparked and inspired me to turn again to texts that have long frustrated me, to recognize that I have agency too. I can put my sanctified thinking cap on and seek different kinds of possibilities in the texts before me. We all can.

What I love most about this book is its invitation to a kind of courageous curiosity. Sometimes it's hard to admit to ourselves that the old ways of telling the story just don't do it for us anymore. We are tired of stories that vilify, condemn, and exclude. We are tired of using "God's love" as a weapon to corral and punish everyone who doesn't resolve the story the way we think they should. We are tired of stories that cram us into boxes rather than pull us out of them.

We want to be better, but we don't always know how to get better. In these distressing times, I often beg for answers. But then I remember that to get better answers, I have to ask better questions. The promise of this book is in the reminder that if we will turn our attention again to the stories that we love, better is available to us.

Brittney Cooper
Rutgers University
Crunk Feminist Collective
Author of *Beyond Respectability: The Intellectual Thought of Race Women*

Featured Artists

It was important to me to include art in *BETTER* that not only corroborates what's written, but that also expands, interrogates, or challenges the ideas put forth. As such, the images in the book are less often illustrative of what is being said in the paragraphs where they are found; instead they are allusive, meant to spark imagination and generate fresh intuitions.

The following two photographers answered the call to share their art and passion for a more just, beautiful, and virtue-filled world with this project. I am tremendously happy to feature their work and point you toward the causes that matter to them so you can support them as well.

Nikole Lim is the Cofounder and International Director of Freely in Hope, a nonprofit organization seeking to restore dignity with survivors of sexual violence by providing educational opportunities and platforms for women to fulfill their dreams. From documenting a widow with leprosy in the jungles of Vietnam to providing scholarships for survivors of sexual violence in Zambia, furthering social justice through the arts has been a vital part of Nikole's vocational journey. By using film and photography, Nikole shifts paradigms on how stories are told, platforming voices of the oppressed—sharing stories of immense beauty arising out of seemingly broken situations. Find more of her work at http://www.nikolelim.com.

Carlton Mackey is an artist and scholar. He is an adjunct professor of Film and Media Studies at Emory University and serves as the Director of the Ethics & the Arts Program and Associate Director of the Ethics and Servant Leadership (EASL) Program at the Emory University Center for Ethics. Mackey is the creator of BEAUTIFUL IN EVERY SHADE,™ a signature brand and grassroots empowerment movement about transcending colonized beauty standards to liberate and celebrate what is beautiful in every human being. Three projects of BEAUTIFUL IN EVERY SHADE are 50

Shades of Black, Typical American Families, and Black Men Smile. Find more of his work at http://carltonmackey.com.

Special thanks to the other artists who made their work available to this project as well, either knowingly or through creative commons copyright. You are appreciated for the better you give us eyes and hearts to see in the world.

Acknowledgments

This project would not exist had it not been for the encouragement and countless hours of conversation with my spouse, partner for life, Leslie Watson Bray, clarifying how we want to show up in the world together.

It would not exist were it not for my children, Jaya, Kari and Melvin IV, giving their daddy the time and mental space to create, while always daring to interrupt just often enough to keep us both reminded exactly where priority lies.

The project would be so much less were it not for the invaluable insight of Tashion Macon (strut AGENCY, Atlanta and Los Angeles), brand guru, friend, and fellow dreamer. The book itself would be a meandering mess (I have a lot of thoughts about everything) were it not for the watchful eye, ear, and talent of my editor, Olivia M. Cloud. And I would be remiss not to mention Chalice Press, in particular Steve Knight, Brad Lyons, and Gail Stobaugh, for taking a risk on all the various ways I wanted to change existing norms.

You may start reading and get the impression that I read and watch broadly. While that's somewhat true, I learned from an old Georgia organic farmer-friend, Skip Glover, "you can't read everything," no matter how much you'd like to. However, what I have sought to develop over the years is the spiritual discipline of listening broadly (those who truly know me know how much of a struggle that can be). Any success I have had in the practice of listening has led to a network of trusted sources and friendships whose sundry and disparate experiences with art, philosophy and spirituality, ethics, meaning, and ideas, I drew upon in the completion of this endeavor. So I would be remiss if I did not acknowledge public intellectuals and journalists like Brittney Cooper, Melissa Harris Perry, Michel Martin and Krista Tippett, whose work has done so much to introduce me to new voices. I also want to express appreciation to friends like David Lamotte, Anthony Smith, Jimmy McGee, Eliacin Rosario-Cruz, Brian Ammons, Troy Bronsink, Mike Morrell, Julie Clawson, Brian McLaren, Patrick Shevlin, Juliette Kaplan, Eugene Russell, Kathy Khang, Lisa Anderson, Michael Wright, Stephen Lewis, and many others for commending and being resonant voices to me that I could engage while completing this project.

In addition to the work of greats like Audre Lorde, Toni Morrison, bell hooks, Martin Luther King Jr., el-Hajj Malik el-Shabazz, and Vincent Harding, there are so many others whose influence on my heart and mind lie just beneath the surface of legal obligation to attribution, but without whom I would never have arrived here. As such, I especially would like to acknowledge the works of Howard Thurman, Chief Si'ahl (Seattle), Malcolm Gladwell, Rainer Maria Rilke, and Alice Walker, whose thoughts undergird the original premise of the book.

Furthermore, I owe an ineffable debt of gratitude to anyone who has shared even a fleeting moment of this life journey with me, names too numerable to mention. Because of you, I am incalculably BETTER.

Introduction

By the time these pages open to the light of day, the experience that birthed them will be at least five years old. One of the challenges of traditional publishing is that it takes so long to bring an idea to print. So honestly, I'm not even sure I still believe all the same things now that I did then.[1] In fact, I hope I don't—which is partly why this book isn't about belief (uncritical certainty) so much as it is about faith (humble confidence) in the power of story to lead us into more *and more* beautiful ways of being human.[2]

Despite my theologically conservative upbringing, I eventually gave up on the notion of unassailable religious certitude, because for all our certainty, we've made a royal mess of things. Set aside for a moment all the wars waged and the lives lost on every inhabited continent in the name of religion, which itself trumps nearly all possible arguments in favor of religion. Start simply with the ignorance religion can so often promote, the unwillingness to entertain new experience or additional information. Move from there to the deep materialism that religion outwardly reviles, yet often hypocritically identifies as a sign of divine favor. Consider, too, the alienation and oppression that arise from dividing the world into a chosen "us" and a wretched "them," which brings us back to this business of waging physical, cultural, psychological, economic, and ecological war on all we consider unlike ourselves. When our sense of right and wrong is so self-serving, what are we—and, perhaps more importantly, our children—left to believe about public morality, economic stability, political integrity, personal safety, legal residency, and financial decency in America?

My first notion was to title this book *Deconstructing Our Myths*, but over time that seemed to put the focus on the wrong part of the exercise. Anyone who grows must, over time, deconstruct the intellectual, emotional, physical, and spiritual scaffolding upon which they have hung their intuitions regarding how things were, are, and should be. I was able to challenge and deconstruct much of my own, having spent several years in nourishing journey alongside faithful friends. Then on some bright, crisp morn in early 2011,[3] I woke up to the realization that "I'm done deconstructing (at least for the moment)." And although story

[1] One example of such evolution can be seen between chapters 3 and 8.

[2] Author Brian McLaren does some very important work on the difference between faith and belief in his book *A New Kind of Christianity* (Jossey Bass, 2008).

[3] Why are epiphanic moments so often recalled as happening in the morning?

already mattered a great deal to me, at that point it seemed even more significant as a means of finding a way forward.

This book is about story as story, not story as illustration. These stories bear within themselves the seeds of their own deconstruction—that is to say, they aren't told like they are the one true interpretation of faith. If you walk away from the sacred myths shared herein with intuitions that are different from those I highlight, then the book has still served its purpose.

I work with story primarily for the sake of my children and all the youth with whom I've interacted over the years as a parent, teacher, and mentor. It matters tremendously to me how I pass along faith to my children. I don't mind that my children will have baggage in their faith development; everyone does. But I'll be damned if they'll end up with *my* baggage. No, literally. If there is something worthy of damnation (which seems to be such a common element in many of the old tellings of faith stories), bequeathing all one's hang-ups to one's progeny sounds like as good a reason to damn someone as any. Is there any more certain way to cripple a generation? To avoid crippling our children, it seems to me one has to begin the deep work of unpacking personal baggage, examining what's in those suitcases and steamer trunks and recognize what has been the compelling factor in carrying these accoutrements this far. The hope is that over time we'll learn how to lay some of that crap down and learn to travel light. I remember reading once about being light in the world . . .

I have heard more than once over the past few years that story is rising to prominence, specifically because people are seeking ways to re-enchant their world. Far be it from me to attempt to re-enchant scripture or the world of which it speaks. However, this is my humble attempt to polish away much of the dross that has obscured from us a world already deeply enchanted, if we only find the eyes to see it.

What I am arguing for is reimagining the way we tell our faith stories—which for me, a follower of Jesus, is the biblical narrative—so that they point to beloved community and beyond. Reimagining, as I use the term, is affirmative critique and adaptive reuse rooted in deep appreciation for the best intuitions of those who came before us. It's an attempt to improve upon, not reject, the past, as I'm not sure one can reimagine out of disdain. So it is saying that, although I may differ with Martin Luther King Jr., preferring a more *active*[4] nonviolent resistance, I wouldn't,

[4] I just think that, if you actively have your foot on my neck, we can't continue in rational conversation until that is rectified, even if that means I have to grab your foot and put you on your butt. As long as you're standing over me it's not a conversation between persons who perceive one another as equals. There's no need to converse about your foot on my neck: that just needs to be remedied.

as many did in the 1950s (including my own grandmother), negatively characterize him as a misguided agitator.

It's also my getting almost to the end of a theology degree and deciding I needed to see if God could be bigger than my tradition. It's having the LGBTQIA kids at my first full-time teaching assignment befriend me long before I was open-and-affirming.[5] It's even hearing then sixty-something year old comedian and activist Dick Gregory explain how he came to terms with his daughter dating a white boy by realizing that he had devoted his life to shaping a world in which young people judged one another by the content of their character, rather than by the color of their skin.[6] I had to die to all these ways of being in order to imagine new possibilities. Where I am now isn't detached from my former self but rather a reimagined version of self.

Reimagining, as I define it, is not the same as just making shit up, finding our own way, or setting our own course. If you think about making things up as sour milk, then reimagining is more analogous to making cheese. Yet, no one calls a cheese maker a heretic, nor those who love cheese blasphemers of milk.[7] Reimagining is actually an attempt to delve more faithfully into the deep wisdom, the best intuitions of our traditions, rather than to extrapolate old metaphors further—creating our own interpretations of previous interpretations (vegan cheese). Attempts to create pop faith stories, symbols, rituals, and celebrations seem to amount to little more than this.

Reimagining is more than mere praise for the sentiment of William Ernest Henley's "Invictus." It doesn't automatically make you "the master of [your] fate . . . the Captain of [your] soul." Reimagining, as espoused herein, is an intergenerational and communal process.[8] It starts with a common point of reference and expounds upon a shared sense of virtue. It's the story of us, not just the story of me.

For Christians, that common point of reference might be the Fruit of the Spirit or the Sermon on the Mount or any of the many other cardinal virtues found in Judeo-Christian scripture. "The fruit of the Spirit [of the Jesus way]," the Apostle Paul wrote to his friends in Galatia, "is love, joy, peace, patience, kindness, generosity, faithfulness, gentleness, and self-control."[9]

Or it might be the words Jesus spoke to a crowd gathered by the Sea of Galilee, "You have heard that it was said, 'You shall love

[5] Language associated with Christian spaces that are "open" to (i.e., safe) and "affirming" of (i.e., promoting the God-given dignity of) LGBTQIA individuals and their families.

[6] Which helped me to resolve my last hang-ups regarding interracial dating.

[7] Although, my wife says, people into vegan "cheese" are proudly heretics and blasphemers of all things dairy.

[8] Life experience has taught me that there are few, if any, original thoughts. And I have become increasingly suspicious of ideas that some elder cannot see the veracity in or of innovations that seek to sever all ties with what came before it. The seeds of the future are found in the past. Even the intuitions espoused in this book are more reclamation than revelation.

[9] Galatians 5:22-23 NRSV

[10] Matthew 5:43-44 NRSV

your neighbor and hate your enemy.' But I say to you, Love your enemies and pray for those who persecute you."[10]

The message Paul wrote to Philippi is a common point of reference as well: "whatsoever things are true, whatsoever things are honest, whatsoever things are just, whatsoever things are pure, whatsoever things are lovely, whatsoever things are of good report; if there be any virtue, and if there be any praise, think on these things."[11]

[11] Philippians 4:8 KJV

Other positive traditions, even irreligious traditions like Humanism, articulate the necessity of this type of ethic in a pluralistic world. I would suggest it is because reimagining is embedded in this type of community and/or shared tradition that it has credibility.

Some may question whether reimagining is the best approach to having better stories. Why not instead start from scratch? They might advocate creating a new, perhaps religiously neutral, mythology through which to communicate our best intuitions. It's an idea.

Take *Star Wars*, for example, a worldwide cinematic phenomenon that spans generations and transcends cultures. Strangely enough, *Star Wars* creator George Lucas, the man religious fanatics once called a Satanist and a corrupter of spiritual imagination, said in a 1980s interview with Bill Moyer that the imagery from his stories shouldn't serve as substitutes for the richness of religious tradition. Rather, he had hoped that his talk of "The Force" and his ability to capture on-screen the hero's adventure and the epic struggle between good and evil would encourage viewers back into their various spiritual traditions.

Religious fundamentalists need not fear. There is little threat of *Star Wars* or *Harry Potter* or other mythological movies destroying our religious institutions any time soon. Scripture isn't going anywhere as a primary influence in the lives of a significant portion of the people on this planet. With only about a billion or so of the estimated seven billion people in the world identifying as irreligious, the value of faith mythology is still intact for now.

[12] "American Nones: The Profile of the No Religion Population," a report based on the *American Religious Identification Survey 2008*, Trinity College, Hartford, Connecticut. Available at https://commons.trincoll.edu/aris/publications/2008-2/aris-2008-summary-report/.

There is, however, some evidence that "no religion" is the fastest growing religious status in the United States.[12] This does not surprise me. In fact, I would argue that continuing to tell stories of faith in the same way is to guarantee they'll be largely discredited as broken certainties of a former time. By reimagining our stories of faith, however, we preserve their value for posterity.

This book is about how to pass faith along to our kids and to others in ways that remain valued, relevant, and useful. In case you've missed it, gone are the days of holding uncritically to what one's parents held as truth. Young people arriving at adulthood may very well abandon the faith of their fathers and mothers. However, if it is not too audacious of me, I think it safe to say that if parents and mentors practice the storytelling demonstrated in this book, they will be more effective at passing along a faith that will be received by future generations. Therefore, a major audience for this book is parents and mentors who know the value of faith, yet recognize that their progeny may not hold faith on the same terms.

This book is not for folks who've figured it all out. If your religious certainty is working for you and yours, by all means, stick with it. Far be it from me to call into question anything life-giving for anyone. If you are fundamentally or foundationally committed to an old-time religion or to the contemporized expression of similar core principles, this book likely will only annoy you and perhaps feel like smoke masquerading as fresh air.[13]

[13] Although I do appreciate the purchase!

However, if you're like so many for whom uncritical certitude is no longer working and you don't know why or what to do about it. If you've seen that while your certainties may privilege you and folk like you just fine, others pay a pretty high cost in maintenance of your privilege and you want to do something to rectify that. Then *BETTER* should feel like oxygen in your lungs.

Whatever your rationale for reading, I hope *BETTER* sparks meaning-filled conversation for you and your faith (or non-faith) community. If so, please make a point of letting me hear about it.

Expository Arc for
BETTER: Waking Up to Who We Could Be

The story of Esther demonstrates sacred mythology isn't culturally intuitive for 21st century post-modern gentiles. So we have to take time to understand the context of any story if we are going to be able to derive credible meaning from it.

The story of Ruth and Hagar demonstrates that ancient culture and the understanding of virtue found therein is far from static, and it quite unmistakably evolves over time.

The stories of Ezra and Nehemiah demonstrate that the protagonists of sacred myths aren't always meant to be emulated, and with certain thematic arcs stretching for generations, we have to see the ripple effects of "hero's" actions before we can judge their value.

ch 5

Beloved community finally shares ownership of the good being created.

ch 4

Beloved community accepts others for how they choose to identify, even as that identity varies across situations.

The story of the Syrophenician woman's encounter with Jesus demonstrates that no sacred myth can be reduced to one eternally salient point.

ch 3

Beloved community lets others tell their own story.

The relational challenges of society reflect the way we've interpreted our sacred myths over time. The COMPOST methodology helps us reimagine these world-changing stories in both the present and the future.

ch 2

Beloved community champions the human dignity of all.

ch 1

MLK's metaphor of beloved community is one of the most prominent modern examples of how good story can change the world for the better. His work inspires us to reengage sacred myth to find what it can teach us about living more beautiful, just and virtue-filled lives.

BETTER develops two complementary lines of thought simultaneously as illustrated below:

(a) there are more beautiful, more just, more virtue-filled ways to tell our stories of faith and possibility.

(b) doing so gives us more beautiful, more just, more virtue-filled ways of being in the world.

The story of Zacchaeus demonstrates that, even when the goal is to tell stories that COMPOST, not every telling of every sacred myth will have all the elements.

ch 6

Beloved community leverages privilege on behalf of others.

The story of David demonstrates sacred myths are not stories that happened once, but stories that happen time and time again. Stories that COMPOST acknowledge patterns, even when they are at odds with Western cultural norms.

ch 7

Beloved community makes room for others.

The story of the woman who washed Jesus's feet offers opportunity to make narrative amends to those historically oppressed by poor tellings of our sacred myths. The COMPOST process, not just COMPOST attributes, moves us in the direction of much needed reparations.

ch 8

Beloved community seeks liberation, not progress, transformation, not just reform.

The story of Moses's journey back to Egypt demonstrates that each generation has to find its own devotion to the stories and rituals of their faith.

ch 9

Beloved community honors the past by improving on it.

While the COMPOST methodology doesn't offer us new certainty, it does give us ears to apprehend fresh intuitions each time we re-tell our sacred myths.

ch 10

Beloved community is possible. However, the arc of the moral universe doesn't bend itself toward justice. We have to bend it, through our telling of better stories and our building of a better world.

What if the world that persists is exactly the world we've storied into existence with the hostile faith stories we tell?

CHAPTER ONE

Better Stories

Shortly after the Supreme Court of the United States 2015 decision to uphold marriage equality as constitutional, a former student of mine posted an affirmation of his faith on Facebook that went something like:

> To my LBGTQ friends, I don't think of you any less because of my growing faith in Jesus and my belief in the teachings of my church. You are human, just like me. Jesus wants me to love ALL people, no matter their walk of life.
>
> Nonetheless, I believe marriage is between a man and a woman and that Satan is attacking that structure. To be honest, I view homosexuality as the Bible defines it—a sin. Yes, there are A LOT of sinful acts I commit daily. This is me making a stand on what is truth as I understand it. I am in no position to condemn anyone, but I do have the right to express my belief.
>
> If knowing this you can't remain friends with me, I'll respect your decision. No hard feelings.

My first reaction was to wonder: How had the story of God been imparted during his formative years that caused this young adult to think of faith as something to be held over and against others? My lament doubled upon reading the comments of yet another young adult who concurred with my former student, rationalizing her refusal to attend, and thus "condone," her sister's upcoming nuptials to a same-sex partner.

Having grown up in the same fundamentalist tradition as these two, I was not befuddled by the theology, nor by the way it was being positioned.

> When children grow up to mimic their parents' hostility toward others, it's often intensified because their actions are that much further removed from the rationale and context that birthed the stories they parrot.

As carefully as I could, so as to not come off as condescending, I shared with the growing number of supportive commentators that in the majority of stories handed down to us Jesus takes an opposite tact. The only exceptions were during his dealings with intransigent and exploitative religio-political leaders. In fact, the accusations deemed most damning in the biblical account are that Jesus consorted with sinners, thus colluding with the devil.

I pressed this point about *the actual Jesus story* across several comments until, in grand Keyser Söze[1] fashion, the young woman intent on snubbing her sister in the name of God dismissed me with the retort: "Satan's greatest weapon is man's ignorance of God's Word."

That social media exchange dismays me on multiple levels, primarily because it uses story—in this instance, the story of God—to justify the oppression of another. Story is the most powerful, yet seemingly innocuous, cultural force on the planet.

There are countless examples of how story is used as a weapon against others. For instance, in the nearly one hundred years since the women's suffrage movement began in the United States, working women more often than we care to admit hit a glass ceiling as they seek to advance their careers, yet we beguile ourselves with stories of "level playing fields." Furthermore, even as the number of female-headed households increases, women take home 72 cents or less for every dollar a man makes doing the same job, but we delude ourselves with tales of "equal opportunity." Four decades after *Roe v. Wade*, women encounter restrictions on contraception, the defunding of women's health initiatives, the redefinition of rape, and the erosion of protections from intimate partner violence. These misogynist policies come at the whim of predominantly male legislative bodies, while many insist there is no gender bias in our laws. Moreover, as our daughters, mothers, sisters, aunts, and nieces rise in school,

in the workplace, and especially the military, so do incidents of sexual assault. Still the story so often told, particularly in conservative faith spaces, is that the outrage committed had something to do with what a woman was wearing or doing.

However, the open hostility in our stories isn't just toward women.

[1] *The Usual Suspects* (MGM, 1995). Most memorable line: "The greatest trick the devil ever pulled was convincing the world he didn't exist."

Although it's been nearly fifty years since Martin Luther King Jr. and his contemporaries shamed overt racism underground, people of color continue to be suspected, arrested, charged, tried, sentenced, and incarcerated at rates that far exceed that of whites for the same crimes. We've been taught to regard these atrocities as "law and order." People of color still lose their lives at the hands of white privilege, based on erroneous assumptions about race. But society works hard to account for it, reaching for inadequate legal designations like "justifiable use of force" or "stand your ground." White border citizens take up arms to repel the migration of destitute minors to our brown south, while ignoring hundreds of miles of unpoliced border to our white north, and the farce we tell is of an unbiased interest in "homeland security."

Nonetheless, stories of such cruelty don't restrict themselves to people of color. Employers that actively solicit government benefits paid for by all taxpayers hire, fire, or deny employment benefits based on sexual orientation or gender expression, justifying their actions as "religious liberty." To give such employers legal cover, across the country conservative state lawmakers vote into law regressive and openly discriminatory laws and have the audacity to name their legislation, "Religious Freedom Restoration Acts." Landlords evict or deny housing to LGBTQIA persons (particularly elders and youth) and call it "protecting property values." Meanwhile, in our schools and neighborhoods, bullies make life a living hell for LGBTQIA kids (particularly transgender and gender nonconforming), pushing many of them to consider taking their own lives. Yet these heinous actions are dismissed as "kids will be kids."

These narratives of oppression haunt us at every turn, as if they are somehow innate parts of the human condition. As if they aren't relational problems seeking relational responses. They reveal a fundamental disconnect between ourselves and others—"us" versus "them"—someone wanting to deny the full humanity of another, while often cloaking that desire in words of religion, faith, and good intent. There must be reasons these disconnects persist despite our best lip service and well wishing to the contrary.

What if the world that persists—with all its racism, sexism, heterosexism, ableism, religious hatred, and ecological

[2] Not to mention poverty, militarism, consolidated wealth, food insecurity, water shortage, barriers to education, and so on—all of which are often justified by popular expressions of religion.

[3] See his magnum opus, *There is a River* (Mariner Books, 1993).

[4] "[Unedited] Vincent Harding with Krista Tippett," On Being with Krista Tippett, February 4, 2011, http://www. onbeing.org/program/ civility-history- and- hope/79.

disregard[2]*—is exactly the world we've storied into existence with the hostile faith stories we tell?*

What is story but a language bridge for conveying ideas from one person or generation to the next? Each of the narratives of oppression cited above contains specific language to communicate particular ideas about whom we value and whom we don't; what we accept and what we won't. How is that not story? It has all the essentials: character, setting, conflict, and plot.

The late civil rights luminary and historian Vincent Harding, who was uniquely gifted at preserving narrative history,[3] suggests,

> [Story] is the way human community has developed over the millennia. . . . Storytellers bring the history of the experience, of the people, of the group, so that those who are new will know where they came from and what their own possibilities and directions might be. My own sense is that there is something deeply built into us that needs story itself. That story is a source of nurture. That we cannot become really true human beings—for ourselves and for each other—without story.[4]

Of Myth and Men

Of course, Harding isn't talking about everyday news reports, tall tales, or children's books, although they play their part. He's talking about those widely known cultural narratives into which nations and ethnicities and religions invest their strongest convictions about the world and their place in it. Literature teachers refer to such stories as myth (which doesn't mean "lie," as many presume). These myths take the form of prose and poetry, song and film, art and ritual passed on from old to young, teacher to student, friend to neighbor. They become the stories around which we organize the thinking and the doing of our daily lives.

Consider, for example, some well-known Christian mythology. Doesn't the story of Adam and Eve *as often recalled* teach us that heterosexual relationships are normative? And doesn't that same story, along with the overwhelming gender bias of the Judeo-Christian scriptures *suggest* that men are first and better suited to lead? Likewise, doesn't the story of Noah and the Ark *as often told* to children teach that some deserve to live and some just don't? Doesn't David and Goliath *as generally remembered* affirm that people who worship the "one true God" are meant to rule? C'mon, even if the curse of Cain or Ham as told by racist slaveholders is a crock,[5] doesn't the subjugation of specific people groups and the ignoring of others throughout the stories contained in the Hebrew Bible *as commonly recounted* at least imply that God is not uncomfortable with privileging some over others based on ethnicity or nationality? Sure they do!

No matter how much I love these stories, I've got to admit the truth. We've all seen them used in exactly these ways. I've personally used them in exactly these ways, and it shames me, because these stories were my refuge when I needed protection from that kind of assault on my own fragile sense of personhood growing up. When peers and adults used to pick on me for being too proper or too smart for my own good, these were the stories that assured me I mattered too.

Like the story of Ishmael thrown from the home of his father Abraham—the so-called Father of the Faithful—to die with his single mother in the desert. God doesn't reject Ishmael and his mom just because his father's wife, Sarah, treats him poorly, and his father can't muster enough courage to face the problem. God fulfills God's promise to make of Abraham's progeny a great nation through whom the earth would be blessed. The first step was helping Ishmael's mom find water in the desert to save their lives and later making a way for both his family and half-brother Isaac's family to come together and prosper in peace (Arabs and Jews) for the good of all those around them. Such stories spoke to me for so many reasons. But then, I turned around and learned to use them to deny others equal assurance.

Notwithstanding, my experience and that of many others who gained encouragement from the biblical narrative suggests the problem isn't our stories; but rather, the way we tell them. Which is to say, the way we interpret them. If you think about it, the sacred mythologies of diverse traditions have, more than any other human artifact, preserved for us a sense that better is possible. There is no richer treasure trove of virtue and wisdom, charity and solidarity, social change and cultural advancement than our sacred myths. Even at times when our houses of worship, our schools, our families, governments, corporations, and media— the institutions that have over the years fancied themselves the

[5] Be reminded at: http://en.wikipedia.org/wiki/Curse_and_mark_of_Cain and http://en.wikipedia.org/wiki/Curse_of_Ham.

keepers of our stories—have fallen into corruption, the stories themselves spoke of better.

Yet no herald can hold a message eternally untarnished. So too, the common telling of our sacred myths has evolved in some good and not-so-good ways. Even when we can't, often our children spot the corruption. They recognize misogyny in our faith stories—and homophobia and xenophobia and classism and tribalism and other forms of lunacy. And many of them are calling bullshit on these lies, as perpetuated at home, at school, at church, and on the airways by politicians and others. There's nothing beautiful or sensible or sacred about these ways of being in the world, and the fact that many kids have figured this out should be a source of great hope.

> "America's seismic demographic shift is upending life in our suburbs, cities and our popular culture. So why are we still clinging to the same stories to make sense of these changes?"
> ~Gene Demby, blogger

Sadly, some young people still don't see these hostile ways of being in the world as the lunacy they are. Perhaps that, more than anything, should scare us into moving toward something better. When children grow up to mimic their parents' hostility toward others, it's often intensified because their actions are that much further removed from the rationale and context that birthed the stories they parrot. They become voters who elect civic leaders who, after witnessing an attack carried out by French, Belgian, and Syrian nationals, espouse restricting the free movement of only Syrians as an appropriate response. Then they become indignant when someone cries "racism," because they don't know how to live with integrity against radicalism in all its forms, including their own.

Sociologist and film critic Gareth Higgins, describes the need for stories that better interpret the best of our faith traditions this way:

> We live at a time when much of institutional [religion, particularly my own faith tradition] Christianity, deserves a reputation for, at best, ignoring the real concerns facing most people; and at worst being complicit in perpetuating a system stacked against the poor, the sick, the marginalized, those who suffer. . . . [People of faith] cannot hope to be the kind of culture-shaping [influence] we aim to be unless we clearly articulate the vision of a new/old kind of [faith] that has captured our hearts.... We live in a cultural context where words and images

matter—as the very currency of human relationships is so influenced, if not now dominated, by words and images (email, Twitter, Facebook; not to mention sermons, lyrics, film scripts, Banksy's art, Obama's campaign posters, and so on). That context demands that we state clearly—with words and images, as well as in our practices—[the hope we hold for a better world].[6]

If we storied ourselves into the way things are, there must be a way to story ourselves out of it. And that's exactly what people are doing. Tom's Shoes donates a pair of shoes to someone who can't afford them every time someone who can afford them buys a pair. Charity Water puts 100 percent of public donations toward clean water projects, by challenging deep-pocket private donors to back their operations costs. Hip Hop Public Health is getting grandparents and parents to seek medical treatment by using hip hop to educate kids on the signs of developing health issues. The City of Salt Lake is impacting homelessness by giving people homes. They've figured out it only costs $11,000 per year to set a homeless person up with an apartment and a social worker, whereas they were spending $16,670 per person annually on ER visits and jail stays. We all know stories that claim these things couldn't be done, but people are doing them successfully. Since religion wouldn't stand up and live out the true meaning of its creed, the people involved in these projects, whether persons of faith or not, have stepped up to tell better stories.

[6] Original write-up about the rationale for a Wild Goose Festival, featured on the festival's website 2011-2014.

The stories of Tom's Shoes, Charity Water, Hip Hop Public Health, and Salt Lake City bridge a supposedly irreconcilable divide woven into our dominant narratives—the divide between haves and have-nots, the divide between profit and purpose, the divide between possible and impossible. These folk didn't wait for religious institutions to get their act together, but that doesn't mean there is no room for people of faith. Who better to come alongside and scale these better ways of being in the world than people of faith who have thousands of years of experience telling life-changing stories?

> "Storytellers bring the history of the experience, of the people, of the group, so that those who are new will know where they came from and what their own possibilities and directions might be."
> -Vincent Harding, civil rights icon and historian

Now don't get it twisted. I recognize that at the moment religious institutions have little credibility as promoters of virtue. It is often religious institutions that promote the injustices recalled at the beginning of this chapter. Nonetheless, faith is the lens through which many people like myself recognize that things are not as they ought to be. Faith gives me hope and a sense of direction for how to move toward the better world I believe is possible. Faith similarly informs the sensibilities of more than half of the seven billion people on the planet. That's 5.5 billion people with the sense that there is an Absolute in the universe with definite designs on a life worth living. There has to be a way to leverage that positive belief for the good of all. People of faith stand in a long line—generations—of people who have labored to live more justly, more virtuously, more beautifully, albeit imperfectly. With so much internal and external motivation, if people of faith can't tell more beautiful stories, who can?

When we revisit the sacred myths of our various traditions, we can yet hear whispers of a deep virtue and even critique that belies the unfailing pro-us-and-our-way-of-life messages we most often take from them. We find persons responding to a call to move beyond personal comfort into a place that brings greater comfort to others. We see ordinary people questing for possibilities that won't exist unless that specific character brings them into being. And if we're astute, we realize such mythic heroism is still possible today. Though handed down for millennia, our faith stories are now ours to tell and live, and we can choose to tell them in new and living ways.

Man of the Century

Reimagining our sacred myths is exactly what Martin Luther King Jr. was doing when, in response to a deeply religious white America that was by and large convinced that its treatment of Negroes honored their Christian faith stories, began to speak of a beloved community. King adopted the language from early twentieth-century philosopher/theologian Josiah Royce, who founded the Fellowship of Reconciliation. The words *beloved community* do not appear in Christian sacred text, but King began to see it as the tangible communal and *political* end to what the stories of Christian scripture, particularly the stories of Jesus, intimated about living nonviolently.

The King Center website documents:

> As early as 1956, Dr. King spoke of The Beloved Community as the end goal of nonviolent boycotts. As he said in a speech at a victory rally following the

announcement of a favorable U.S. Supreme Court Decision desegregating the seats on Montgomery's busses, "the end is reconciliation; the end is redemption; the end is the creation of the Beloved Community. It is this type of spirit and this type of love that can transform opponents into friends. It is this type of understanding goodwill that will transform the deep gloom of the old age into the exuberant gladness of the new age. It is this love which will bring about miracles in the hearts of men."[7]

King's use of images like "beloved community" captured onlookers' imaginations and catapulted him onto a world stage. Who in their right minds wouldn't want to belong to the world about which King dreamed? I know when I heard it I wanted to. You mean to tell me that there is a way to be in the world that people of goodwill in all their glorious differences—the fifty-two-year-old Caucasian banker, the twenty-five-year-old indigenous entrepreneur, the seventeen-year-old transgender Asian American homeschooler, the thirty-three-year-old Latino immigrant soldier and I—could connect with each other and together rewrite the stories of oppression in the world? Sign me up!

King would later express, "[Beloved community is] the aftermath of nonviolence. . . so that when the battle's over, a new relationship comes into being between the [formerly] oppressed and the [former] oppressor.""[8] "I do not think of political power as an end. Neither do I think of economic power as an end. They are ingredients in the objective that we seek…. That objective is a truly brotherly society, the creation of the beloved community."[9]

King began to tell a better story. In beloved community, the story of Adam and Eve is not a story of exclusion and bias, but rather of the radical inclusion of all God's good creation.[10] In beloved community, the story of Noah and his ark is not the story of God's destruction of sinners, but rather of God's saving grace to all creation.[11] In beloved community, the story of David and Goliath is not about God facilitating the triumph of a favorite few over all others, but instead about the historically marginalized and undervalued finding honor in society as well.

[7] Martin Luther King Jr., "Facing the Challenge of a New Age," speech given December 3, 1956, in Montgomery, Alabama, http://www.thekingcenter.org/king-philosophy.

[8] Palm Sunday Sermon on Mohandas K. Gandhi, March 22, 1959.

[9] July 13, 1966 article in *The Christian Century* magazine.

[10] Check out my take on the Adam and Eve Saga—http://findourselves.blogspot.com/search/label/Adam%20and%20Eve.

[11] Hear my take on the Noah Saga—http://findourselves.blogspot.com/search/label/Noah.

> "Discrediting old myths without finding new ones to replace them erodes the basis for common action that once bound those who believed into a public body, capable of acting together."
> -William H. McNeill, historian

King was undoubtedly ahead of his time, and America despised him for it—first by killing him, then by trying to dismiss his genius, then going further by attempting to domesticate or misappropriate his legacy.[12]

Vast numbers of people are waking up to the damage our lesser stories have done to the world and are seeking a script that makes beloved community possible. But you can't wake up to something nearly sixty years after the fact and expect nothing to have changed. Conditions on the ground and in our psyches aren't the same as they were in 1956. There are things we know now that we couldn't know then about our individual and collective selves—the systems and structures of empire in which we intra- and inter-relate, the histories of movements to transform those systems and the lengths to which supremacy will go to maintain itself within whatever iteration of the system comes into being. Beloved community can still be our chosen image of political justice, and sacred myths like David and Goliath can still inspire social change,[13] but our understanding of those metaphors and myths must expand.

As I've noted in previous writing,[14] mythologist Joseph Campbell (the scholar whose ideas inspired the modern myth *Star Wars*) suggests that if our metaphors and myths are to continue to fulfill their vital functions as time passes, they must continually evolve. Metaphors and myths that haven't progressed simply do not address the realities of contemporary life. It's like looking at a very old map of where you currently live. The map may not have on it your home or half the places you go on a regular basis. The map isn't wrong per se, but it is not very useful in helping you orient yourself. Even if you were to recognize a landmark or two as you looked at the map, you'd have to constantly explain to yourself where that landmark is in relation to other places you know. "A mythological image that has to be explained to the brain is not working."[15]

What is necessary to make a mythological image such as beloved community or Adam and Eve or Noah and the ark work for our post-modern/post-colonial[16] brains are not a mere updating of the imagery employed, which we often find in "contemporary churches," but also an acknowledgment, if only tacit, of what we know better since the image was first employed. All too often we try to use old images to justify or idealize "the way things were," ignoring that the "good ol' days" weren't so good for everyone.

[12] See chapter 8.

[13] Check out Malcolm Gladwell, *David and Goliath: Underdogs, Misfits, and the Art of Battling Giants* (New York: Little, Brown and Company, 2013).

[14] *Faith Forward*, ed. Dave Csinos and Melvin Bray (Kelowna, British Columbia: Wood Lake, 2013).

[15] *The Hero's Journey: The World of Joseph Campbell*, 1987, David Kennard and Janelle Balnicke, directors..

[16] After modernity or after colonization. A way of being in the world different from, yet informed by, what came before it.

Take, for example, the traditional imagery of the subservience of women to men. Whereas gender equity still may have been up for debate among civil rights leaders in the 1960s, we now know there's no room for inequality in beloved community. Failure to acknowledge this truth undermines one's credibility. To speak of "traditional family values" as those taught by the Bible in ancient times minimizes the damage done in the name of those values and flies in the face of all the progress that's been made since.

A look back into the biblical narrative will reveal stories wherein traditional values were subverted in favor of a beloved community that enfranchised everyone regardless of gender. The mythological image itself then becomes more recognizable to our post-colonial brains, and we have reason to be interested in what else the story may have to say. It's not that the world has no use for faith stories that challenge our predispositions; it simply has no use for faith stories that set us back.

Beloved community is a beautiful hope and an important corrective on the telos of our faith stories. But like many mythological images before it, beloved community (and all the tangible, affirmative tactics and vision associated with it) can also be co-opted, corrupted, or rendered useless over time. What is needed is not just better language that speaks of a more worthy end, but a better way to preserve and create new meaning on our journey toward that end.

> "The Bible cannot go unchallenged in so far as the role it has played in legitimating the dehumanization of people of African [and other] ancestry in general and the sexual exploitation of women of African [and other] ancestry in particular. It cannot be understood as some universal, transcendent, timeless force to which world readers in the name of being pious and faithful followers must meekly submit. It must be understood as a politically and socially drenched text invested in ordering relations between people, legitimating some viewpoints, and delegitimizing other viewpoints."
> ~Renita Weems, womanist scholar

Nature's way of doing this is called composting. As a part of the life cycle, the organic remnants of that which is no longer alive and vital is broken down into its constituent parts and used as nutrient for the next generative organism emerging. This is the way life continues: That Which Is gives its life to make way for That Which Is Becoming. The only organics that don't regenerate into nourishment for what is coming next are those that become petrified and serve only as windows into the past, rather than vital contributors to the present.

There are some stories, myths that do the same (e.g., the stoning of adulterous women in the Bible or speaking of communities of faith as if they were conquering armies). Joseph Campbell would often refer to these as "petrifacts."

What if we discern other ways to tell faith stories—even those we've begun to tell through a beloved community lens—so that the specific interpretations, forms, and metaphors used don't become calcified in our imaginations? Wouldn't the world be better if each of us took the time to find better ways of holding our faith stories in it?

Psycho-Degradable Stories

A masterful storyteller and friend Russell Rathbun once set out with me to see if we could identify the elements of stories that are life-giving to our imaginations for a time, yet easily "psycho-degrade" when they are no longer useful. We called them "stories that compost."

We concluded that stories that COMPOST:

<u>C</u>onfess far more than they proscribe. Have you ever noticed how much religion is about what will happen, should happen or is happening with people other than ourselves? It seems to me that proscriptions about others are far more likely to fester into *petrifacts* than our confessions about ourselves, because when we speak about ourselves we never want to leave the story at its low point. We are always anxious to tell the rest.

Put <u>O</u>pposing forces in dynamic with each other. There is a tendency in the telling of religious stories to reduce them to, "There was mess. God came. Whomever lived happily ever after. The end." We know, however, that's not the way life is. There's a lot of doubt and loss and uncertainty with which we have to reckon—God or not. So why not tell stories full of the dialectical tension of life? Why make an idol out of our particular understanding of God—especially when theists know that an encounter with the true and living God seldom resolves tension; more often than not God's interference heightens it.

Have the <u>M</u>eekness to admit other interpretations—even in the midst of telling the story. I've found that the best way to start to get at this is to begin to pepper one's storytelling with phrases like "maybe," "perhaps," "on the other hand," "as best I understand," "as far as I can tell," "one way of looking at it might be," "the way the story has been handed down to us." By moving away from absolute proclamations, we make room for others to have something to say too.

Pose questions more than answers. Conceptually, faith (humble confidence) is more analogous to questions than to answers. Questions create relationship because they draw people into conversation, setting them on a journey together. Questions drive us toward people we may have never otherwise engaged. If we let them, questions move us away from antagonism to care for one another.

Nurture Others-interestedness. Have you ever wondered why the virtues lauded by most faith traditions are so very communal? Either they seek the good of others or foster an environment that can't wait to be shared. Even Christian imagery like "Fruit of the Spirit" calls to mind the fact that trees share their fruit; otherwise, the fruit spoils. This is what makes a faith story a story of faith: humble confidence in the mystery that though virtue costs our all, instead of diminishing us, fills our lives with an overflowing richness.

Choose Susceptibility to harm. Someone obviously thought they could improve on the Jesus story (the biblical narrative leading up to it and the narrative flowing from it) by recasting it as the grand and glorious triumph of good over evil. "Mine eyes have seen the glory of the coming of the Lord. He is trampling out the vintage where the grapes of wrath are stored. He has loosed the fateful lightning of his terrible swift sword. His truth is marching on!"[17] Whereas I get the need to rally the weary, there is nothing about the Jesus story that is this triumphal. It is a story fraught with vulnerability that subverts the triumphant; and that's where its power lies.

[17] Julia Howe, "Battle Hymn of the Republic," 1861.

Treat Tradition as a living word—a bell that is ringing, not a bell that has rung. A tradition cannot be alive and not change. So then, by their nature, COMPOSTable stories are filled with grace and resurrection—unafraid to converse (not engage in parallel monologuing) with that which heretofore had not been encountered.

Once we identified the types of stories that sustain life, we then wanted to discover if others also found it helpful to recount their sacred myths in this way. We took groups through a reading of a common scripture narrative with these six simple instructions:

1. Read the passage for what it says and doesn't say.

2. How have you traditionally heard this story told?

3. List three things you love about the passage as you are now reading it.

4. List three things that have bugged you about the story itself or the way the story is typically recounted.

5. Articulate three questions that come to mind when you think of this story.

6. Now, select one thing from each of the three preceding categories, and use them to reimagine the story keeping in mind the seven attributes of stories that COMPOST.

For the purpose of this book, which is *to show how reimagining our faith stories reshapes our way of being in the world,* I will add a seventh step: "What intuitions arise from our telling of the story that point us toward beloved community?" In each chapter I'll name what I smell. It's perfectly okay if you smell something totally different. The goal isn't unanimity; but rather, to tell stories that celebrate our current best intuitions until we develop better ones.

When told this way, our reimagined faith stories bear within themselves the seeds of their own deconstruction—that is to say they aren't told as if they are the one true and eternal interpretation. The credibility of usefulness within a specific context is sufficient, particularly if we are ready to admit that, even taking the most favorable view, we are simply doing the best we can with what we know at the moment. The essential part is that, instead of mistaking our interpretive intuitions for the virtues they help us imperfectly make sense of, we should insist the intuitions derived from our storytelling always affirm the virtues that gave rise to them (love, joy, peace, patience, gentleness, meekness, self-control, courage, and so on). And when the imperfections of our intuitions become more pronounced than the beauty of the virtue they're supposed to teach us, let's give ourselves and others, especially our children, permission to reimagine anew.[18]

So then, the story of Adam and Eve isn't just about the radical inclusion of all God's good creation in honor of our hopes for beloved community. The story is about any and every generative interpretation that can be found that helps meet the needs of the present without compromising our capacity for interpreting the story in more beautiful, more just, and more virtue-filled ways in the future.

[18] *Faith Forward,* ed. Dave Csinos and Melvin Bray (CopperHouse, 2013).

Last Rights

People of religious upbringing may have inhibitions about playing (in the best sense of the word) with sacred text this way. Freedom to embrace reimagining as a viable recourse may be linked to a few realizations. The first is something Rathbun said the first time we facilitated together: "You can't break scripture. And you shouldn't be afraid to. It's not 'precious.'" Shocking, I know, but let it settle in. Scripture is not a thing to be coveted and possessed, like Gollum lusting over the One Ring in *Lord of the Rings*. It doesn't need our protection. It is only the story of people just like us trying to figure it all out. In fact, this idea of reimagining our sacred myths is as old as religion itself.[19] Any way scripture can be used to help us find our way forward is valid.

Secondly, there is no neutral telling of any story. As US Supreme Court Justice Sonia Sotomayor famously posited during her confirmation hearing, we—and our stories—are products of our unique personal experiences. Snow White's "Mirror, mirror on the wall, who's the fairest of them all?" is not innocuous.[20] It affirms certain things many people of European descent want their children to believe about themselves. Unfortunately, it also condemns, even if inadvertently, all who do not neatly fit into the limited categories it establishes for what is "fair," especially when told within a culture that is insistent on maintaining those categories. So what happens when the story of Mary, mother of Jesus, has been recast to resemble Snow White, Sleeping Beauty, or Cinderella? What do we mistakenly sanctify that we shouldn't? What do we universally incriminate that we mustn't? Might I suggest it is far and away time to renew our minds with honest images of those we pronounce as heroes of our faith and the times in which they lived?

Thirdly, we can't do any worse to our faith traditions or our world than already has been done. As I read to my three children from the series and authors with which I grew up, I found myself in the awkward position of trying to rewrite on the fly the inane triumphalism that infects the stories that brought me to faith—stories like Israel's needlessly hostile and self-righteous conquest of the Canaanites and the expectation of many Christians that Jesus's Second Coming will somehow more resemble a similar triumph over all other religions rather than the peace and goodwill

> "The system under which we now exist has to be radically changed. This . . . means facing a system that does not lend itself to your needs and devising means by which you change that system."
> ~Ella Baker, community organizer

[19] Within Judaism, in addition to gleaning metaphors from other faiths (see chapter 10), reimagining has taken other forms, for instance, by spawning new interpretive traditions (for example, Midrash and Targum). Within Christianity, although we don't always think of them as such, each Christian denomination is, in effect, an alternate interpretive tradition. In the first split, the upstart Catholic interpretive tradition broke away from the Orthodox tradition. Approximately five hundred years later, the Catholic Church split over who was the rightful pope, the one in France or the one in Rome. Then about five hundred years later, Martin Luther nailed his ninety-five theses to the door of the cathedral in Wittenberg, and the Protestant Reform interpretive tradition was born. There have been several lesser denominational splinterings among Protestants since, but if we remain true to form, according to author Phyllis Tickle, it's about time for us to clean out our theological attic once again.

[20] Both 2012 cinematic versions (*Mirror, Mirror* and *Snow White and the Huntsman*) end with the notion that the only way forward involves violence against our elders!

[21] In the a conference I helped host about passing faith on to children in the current age (Children, Youth, and a New Kind of Christianity, 2012, Washington, D.C.), Brian McLaren lamented for his own grandchildren that with the influx of Christians into politics, we have brought the very low level, even toxic, discourse so common in churches into the public sphere. "Defamation, half-truth, exaggeration, it's just part of preaching, and it's very acceptable in religious settings. You don't have to be fair when talking about the devil—anything goes. So [with a politics saturated with actors from this background] . . . we're dealing with the [very real] possibility . . . that Christians will blow up the world. The most likely people to create the next Holocaust are Christians. The most likely people to press the button that drops nuclear bombs are Christians. And if not that, the most likely people to have the next BP oil spill were people who are 'praising Jesus's on Sunday and filing false inspection reports on Monday. And the people who are going to make sure we don't deal with global climate change are Christians. We've got stuff in our religion that, if we keep people in churches

of his first advent. Just because someone wrote a battle hymn for America with the lyrics, "He is *trampling* out the vintage where the grapes of *wrath* are stored." doesn't make that the script by which God is playing.

Moreover, I am embarrassed by my children's insightful questioning as to whether Moses or Esther, Mary or Jesus actually were like their mid-century, pro-Anglo, pro-West depictions. There are only so many times the response, "That is just one person's imagination," can cover the multitude of transgressions that have been committed in the name of those images—the people alienated, the wars justified, the masses condemned, the atrocities committed, and the absurdities perpetuated.

It's as true for Christianity as it is for other religions. I stand appalled at how bad a PR job Christians typically do for Jesus. Not only can our wading in to add our might not do any worse, it may be the only thing that can do any better. People of faith, our children, and our children's children living out of better intuitions is the only form of apology anyone on the receiving end of our previously hostile stories wants to hear.

The fourth and perhaps most important realization is that we are not alone. As we arrive at these realizations about the power of story and the chance for beloved community, there are tens of thousands finally feeling free to make their faith stories their own enough to use them to change the world, instead of surrendering them to the most strident voices among us.[21] For example, instead of being paralyzed by the contemporary American myth of the Muslim threat, New Yorker Linda Sarsour, a young Muslim mother and fierce social justice advocate, went door to door with Muslim friends in the aftermath of Hurricane Sandy offering neighbors hot pies of pizza while they were without gas and were pumping water out of their homes. Instead of being immobilized by the conservative story of gay wimpishness and illegitimacy, Josh Lesser, an extraordinarily generous same gender-loving rabbi in Atlanta, put his own body in harm's way to protect the ceremonial fishing rights of indigenous neighbors. Josh locked arms with sympathizers to form a human chain around the place where his neighbors were fishing, thus taking the brunt of the taunts and physical abuse from conservative white locals seeking to disrupt the ritual. Instead of sitting comfortably in and being comforted by a public narrative of white supremacy, Hannah Bonner, a self-identified privileged white Methodist minister stood vigil along with friends for eighty days at the Waller County, Texas, sheriff's department where Sandra Bland was imprisoned under false pretenses and murdered. Because to Hannah, Black Lives Matter.

When you think you are alone, it's easy to doubt yourself, to suppress your questions, to wonder if you're the only one who seems not to be able to get with the program of whatever fundamentalism, religious or otherwise, you've been told to buy into. But you and I are not the only ones.[22] Your questions are valid. Your concerns are necessary. The tree of faith must be refreshed from time to time with the waters of doubt, inquiry and reimagination. The fruit of that tree is for the healing of all that divides us[23]. Some might question the importance of lions lying down with lambs[24], but I suspect that the only way we get to the world of which our noblest virtues speak is together.

There are definitely more beautiful, more just, more virtue-filled ways of being in the world than those described at the beginning of this chapter, and most of us know it. Perhaps we just didn't know how to get there. Maybe this idea of telling better faith stories is as good a place to start as any.

Who knows? If people of faith dare to tell better stories, perhaps faith will be something our children have reason to care about in the future.

replicating the kind of faith being passed down in many places, we [will find ourselves] on the wrong team."

[22] I promise, I have met others of all stripes; this is not a Christian-Bale-raspy-voice-Batman thing, "Now there's two."

[23] "Then he showed me a river of the water of life, clear as crystal…. On either side of the river was the tree of life, bearing twelve kinds of fruit, yielding its fruit every month; and the leaves of the tree were for the healing of the nations." (Revelation 22:1–2, NASB).

[24] "The wolf and the lamb will graze together, and the lion will eat straw like the ox; and dust will be the serpent's food. They will do no evil or harm." (Isaiah 65:25, NASB).

CHAPTER TWO

An Inkling about Equity

Clocks are the bane of my existence. One Christmas, my wonderful wife proposed buying me an analog clock that had all the numbers jumbled up in the bottom right-hand quarter between three and six, as if having fallen out of place, with the caption "Whatever, I'm late anyways."

I'm just slow. I talk slowly. I read slowly. I write slowly. I move slowly. It also doesn't help that I don't feel the sense of urgency other people do as time ticks by. I can lose twenty minutes without batting an eye. It takes me an hour and a half to leave the house in the morning if I have to iron and shower. And don't let one of my kids be up to distract me!

My battle with the clock is never more frustrating than on timed tests. I can't stand them because they don't measure what we assume they do. Timed writing tests don't measure how well one writes. They measure how well one writes quickly, which is a different matter. Timed math tests don't measure how well someone understands mathematical concepts. They measure how accurately someone can recall certain math facts quickly.

I was in fifth grade when I learned this lesson all too well. We used to do these one-minute drills over multiplication tables. There were thirty problems on one sheet. Papers were distributed face down. Pencils down. Ready. Set. Go! 7 x 9 = 63, 8 x 4 = 32, 2 x 11 = 22, and so on.

I had known my multiplication facts cold up to 12 x 12 since fourth grade, but I wrote slowly. Still do. I care how my letters are formed. On the other hand, John and Jerry, who nearly always finished first, had handwriting that, as the old folks used to say, looked like chicken scratch. When we would switch papers to grade, they would be half in, half out of their chairs the whole time arguing with the persons grading their sheets and lobbying the teacher that what looked like a 3 really was a 2 or vice versa.

With the practice of this daily ritual, I eventually got faster, and on rare occasion finished an entire sheet. Nonetheless, I learned to accept that I wasn't one of the fast guys. I could live with that. That is, until our teacher announced that she was forming new math groups. It didn't take but a second to notice that all the fast kids were being grouped together—those who scored 25 or more on their minute drills on a consistent basis. Okay. Such is life.

Then it was announced that the fast group would be on an accelerated track for math. With that, I was fuming! I was convinced I should be in that group. "But then again," I argued to myself, "the teacher is an adult, an authority. She obviously has her reasons. She undoubtedly knows more than I. She knows me. She knows what I'm capable of. I'll just let it go."[1]

Now I may not be fast, but I am a natural-born teacher. I'm good too. I have a bona fide Emmy® sitting on my bookshelf, attesting to my feats as a teacher on a local homework help program—which honestly says nothing about my teaching ability. But go on and admit it, for a split second you were impressed.

As young people, we pick up on things about each other intuitively, sometimes long before we can name our own strengths, so we gravitate toward peers who can help us in particular situations. "I want Jaya on my ball team. I talk to James about my problems. I hang with Kari at lunch." Well, I was the guy who could explain things. So when some of the accelerated math folks didn't get how to do something, guess who they would ask to explain it, even though I might have been a chapter or two behind them?

Of course, it doesn't matter now (or does it?), and I'm none the worse for wear (or am I?). But I'd love to know what it is about us that, even when we are free to do otherwise, we structure, settle for or fight tooth-and-nail to preserve systems that legitimize some while delegitimizing others based on criteria of such little consequence.

[1] Add to the scenario the complication that I was the only kid the others in the class knew was black (including possibly the teacher) and that, come to find out later in life, the other few kids of color in the school had similar stories to tell, and math groupings get a little less innocent.

"It is our duty to fight for our freedom."

"Who Are the People in Your Neighborhood?"

> I was shocked that most of the conversation was about "tolerating" and "including" homosexuals within the Church. . . . I don't want to be "allowed" to be part of the Christian faith. I want folks to have read James Baldwin for more reasons than one.[2]

Chris Rose wrote these heartfelt words reflecting upon the time she and her business[3] and life partner, Charlotte Rose, accepted an invitation to attend the inaugural Wild Goose Festival in Shakori Hills, North Carolina, in 2011. What is extraordinary about their attendance is that neither Chris nor Charlotte has any particular affinity to Christianity. Their sense of faith is much more widely informed. Charlotte explains:

> I grew up with my American mother, British father, and two younger brothers in Hong Kong, before the Chinese handover. I attended an international school and frequently traveled all over the world as a young girl. I remember being asked to do an assignment in school about God, upon returning to London at eleven years old, to which I raised my hand in class and quite earnestly inquired, "Which God?"

> I cannot overestimate the spiritual influence of my global travels as a child. At the earliest ages I witnessed people of many cultures worshipping the divine, from Buddhist temples in Thailand to Episcopal churches in California. My own spiritual practice has been driven by a global perspective and curiosity about the many paths of faith.

Christine grew up in a secular, suburban Philadelphia family. As a kid she attended Presbyterian church but never returned after she and her sisters got up in the middle of service and walked out during a sexist sermon about divorce. She studied religion in college, has learned multiple traditions of meditation, and has read the major books of all major world religions. Christine chooses to study and learn from as many sources of wisdom as possible. She recently shared, "I heard a radio sermon the other day encouraging 'believers' to only seek counsel from other Christian believers. To me, this is sacrilege—I have had the blessing of profound counsel

[2] Letters quoted in this section are from Chris and Charlette Rose to the author.

[3] www.pleasuremechanics.com

> Truth can withstand the repeated scrutiny of those who disagree.

from people of so many faith backgrounds. I believe that to limit yourself to fear-based spiritual segregation is an act of hate, not of any love or faith I recognize.'

Our current spiritual practices include sitting meditation, exchanging massage, focused breath-work and spending time outdoors appreciating God's creations. More importantly, we bring our spiritual principles into our relationships. We focus on building authentic relationships with our family and friends, practicing daily acts of service, generosity, praise and reverence. We have sat hospice with many of our dying elders, tending to those we love with our full attention. We throw fabulous parties to celebrate milestones of those we love. We grow and cook food as an act of devotion. We practice radical generosity with our time and attention. It is in these acts of relationship that we practice our devotion to God.

Because of the gracious manner in which Charlotte and Christine communicate, I wanted to assume they came from a Christian background. Upon retrospection, perhaps their lack of background in Christian circles may have contributed to their ability to conjure a completely non-judgmental atmosphere that solicited open conversation from so many participants. In doing so, they were able to help us confront some really important stuff.

Christine later commented on why she and Charlotte found it important to risk in such an unfamiliar setting:

"My big interest . . . [as] we spoke about at our impromptu three-hour workshop on Saturday . . . is that we ALL need to talk about the shame, guilt and fear that we have learned about our sexuality. We need to confront the amount of violence we have suffered as a sexual culture. Healing sexuality in our communities is much more about men, women and families, about respect for the body, than it is about [buzzwords like] "homosexuality" or "sodomy." This is my interest in conversation with what you describe as "recovering fundamentalist" communities.

So many of us share the same vision and values, but are mired by fear and suspicion. We believe that the common spiritual wellness of humanity depends much upon how well we deal with difference. Hostile tolerance is not our vision for inclusion. Rather, we strive for reverent humility, wherein we can learn from the "other" with a passionate curiosity and profound love for the common humanity in us all.

Christine and Charlotte taught me a lot about courage and grace—not to mention sex (all three, unlike the speed of my multiplication, matters of considerable consequence). However, our interaction easily could have been otherwise. With all the fear, suspicion, and delegitimization LGBTQIA persons often endure from people of faith just for *being*—let alone if they dare to presume they have some contribution to make—it's no wonder many want nothing to do with so many "believers." Who should willingly subject themselves to that kind of abuse?

> "As we begin to recognize our deepest feelings, we begin to give up, of necessity, being satisfied with suffering and self-negation, and with the numbness which so often seems like their only alternative in our society. Our acts against oppression become integral with self, motivated and empowered from within."
> ~Audre Lorde, womanist scholar and activist

Guess Who's Coming to Dinner?

Consider this two thousand-year-old story. This is not the traditional interpretation, though it fits the details handed down to us in scripture. I'm inclined to tell the story this way because this telling fits the beloved community we seek and is non-dogmatic enough to be reimagined as need arises.

The woman's steps had mirrored theirs for the last two or three miles. Furtively, she had searched the shadows for courage. Even now she wasn't sure she had found any, but her fear of a missed opportunity had risen to such a fevered pitch that she had to act to halt the screeching in her inner ear. Plus, she couldn't imagine returning home empty-handed. Her daughter needed more help than she herself was able to give.

There was still considerable distance between her and them. There they were on the other side of the market in tight conspiracy, making it awfully difficult for others to get close to their rabbi. He was theirs. They would protect him. Carts and horses, businesses and people, and commerce crowded the street so that she could only catch glimpses from where she stood.

In addition to the physical barriers, she also was separated by social strata. The caste of those who followed Jesus, the one to whom she wanted to speak, were in some circles—in her circles—considered common, dim-witted, dull. Still, that didn't compare to her outsider status. She was Syrophoenician, despised by Jews for her otherwise privileged status as a Roman citizen.

But that couldn't have been the only thing. There was something else about her that made them feel she was indisputably less-than, a displeasure even to God. As a Greek from the Phoenician province of Syria, under Roman law she had the right to compel any random Jew on the street to carry things for her or give her his coat, and so on. Under normal circumstances, her elevated social status would have been despised but held inviolate, particularly in relation to Jews. Her perceived illegitimacy must not have been a condition of law but rather of public perception. Maybe she was a prostitute[4] or a single mother, either of which might have given Jesus's disciples a sense of moral superiority. Or perhaps she was of mixed heritage; yes, a half-breed! If there was anything worse than being Gentile, it was being a half Jew. Her mother would have been considered a traitor, her father unclean, and she despised for her impurity—which, ironically, gave her access to the very privilege that exploited Jews on a daily basis. Jesus's disciples were often looked down upon by class-conscious Jewish elites, but now, here was someone whom even they were considered better than.

She had made her approach front on. She had run a bit ahead, then made a U-turn, and zeroed in on Jesus walking at the head of the pack. It was the only way to get to him.

"Jesus," she started, reaching for his outer robe as his guardians moved to put more than an arm's distance between her and him, "my daughter is desperately ill. Please have mercy on us."

What a strange thing to ask! "Mercy" assumes far more generosity than persons from whom mercy must be begged usually extend. There must have been something different about Jesus that labeled him as one inclined toward mercy. Something in his aspect or in his eyes that suggested the answers to questions of power were different when directed toward him.

Perhaps it was like meeting the Dalai Lama and basking in the compassion in which he walks. So counterintuitive. Particularly considering that the Dalai Lama has been exiled from his beloved home, Tibet, since the 1950s, when he was deposed by the Chinese government for maintaining Tibet's national independence. And what does he advocate toward those who seek his demise, those who maintain his illegitimacy? Unfailing compassion, the same as he advocates toward everyone.

[4] The go-to dismissal of women in the Bible.

It is with this same compassion that Jesus looked into the face of the woman who possessed, to use the words of author Alice Walker,

> a face in which the fever of suffering had left an immense warmth, and the heat of pain had lighted a candle behind the eyes. It sought to understand, to encompass everything, and the struggle to live honorably and understand everything at the same time, to allow for every inconsistency in nature, every weird possibility and personality, had given it a weary serenity that was so entrenched and stable it could be mistaken for stupidity. [That face] made [Jesus] want to love. It made [him] want to weep. It made [him] want to cry out to the young [wo]man to run away, or at least warn [her] about how deeply [she] would be hurt.[5]

I want to believe that Jesus was immediately moved with compassion toward this woman. I also want to believe Jesus saw this as a teaching moment, which gives purpose to what happens next. Surgeons can't heal without first wounding. So that's how I interpret the rest of the story.[6]

So there's Jesus, abruptly confronted by yet another opportunity to do what he's undoubtedly inclined to do. And this strange woman, who is not necessarily one who can lay claim to him or his revolution, is in need. Then there are Jesus's followers, many of whom have left everything in the hope that his rebellion against Rome would take them off the political bottom and put them on top. And, for reasons they can't fully articulate, Jesus's followers despise this woman, who represents everything they long to see come crashing down.

Jesus was undoubtedly aware of their feelings. Contempt, even unarticulated contempt, is as palpable as compassion (which is why it is disingenuous to feign that hate isn't a motive just because it hasn't been explicitly expressed). Clearly, the prospect of an outsider benefiting from that which had benefited them was hard for Jesus's disciples to stomach, and they sought to divert him quickly. One of them, likely Peter, whispered in his ear, "Send her away. She's drawing way too much attention to us."

They had spent more time with him than anyone. Why could they not see? Jesus wondered aloud, "I was sent only to the lost sheep of the house of Israel?"

[5] A description penned by Alice Walker about the character of a movie in her novel *Meridian* (Harcourt Brace Jovanovich, 1976), 190.

[6] There are others who see what happens as Jesus, in a moment of real humanity, getting his hat handed to him, as it were. Still others see his next comments as some sort of statement of the importance of a laser-focused life in achieving a desired impact. There are contextual reasons why I opt for the interpretation I do, but all virtuous imaginations are welcome.

His mind went to Third Isaiah, the interminable school of prophetic defiance. He had read from their writings publicly at the start of his campaign and claimed it as his manifesto, "The Spirit of the Lord is upon me, for it has anointed me to give good news to the poor . . . to set free those in prison, to heal the brokenhearted and to restore sight for the blind, to liberate the oppressed and to proclaim the acceptable year of the Lord!" Why did his own want to fight this?

Things had to change, so Jesus offered the woman the one response that would make the difference, "It doesn't make sense to throw the children's bread to the dogs."

What? Did Jesus just call this woman a dog? No! Not Jesus too! Not my Jesus!

I always told my students that context shapes meaning. So when Pat Buchanan speaks of protecting the future of "white America," it's not the same as when Khalil Gibran Muhammad speaks of preserving the dignity of "black America." Moreover, it means something that those who perpetrated 9/11 are remembered as Muslim terrorists, yet Timothy McVeigh, the Ku Klux Klan, and Christopher Columbus aren't remembered as "Christian terrorists" for the many more they killed in the name of their religious beliefs.

Context can turn a statement into a question. Context can make presumptions of affirmation into sarcasm. Context can flip an old metaphor on its head, making its younger sibling, irony, the better teacher.

Jesus's statement must have warmed the cockles of his disciples' hearts. They were the dear "children" Jesus referenced. The "Children of Israel," heirs to the promise made to Abraham— that through him all the people of the earth would be blessed. Impure, indecent mongrels like this woman were merely unpleasant reminders of the compromises for which the Children of Israel had been given over by God into occupation.

"Good for Jesus to finally acknowledge this," I can hear his disciples thinking. It was just further proof that he was the Messiah. And when he became king, as his inner circle they would be the authorities who could put all these outsiders, these naysayers, these mongrels, in their place.

But Jesus's statement seemed to have the opposite effect on the woman from Syria. Maybe it was a twinkle in Jesus's eye as he stared intently into hers while speaking. Maybe she heard his statement as a question, not a dismissal. Or maybe she just enjoyed matching wits. Whatever the case, she held her own, responding, "True enough, yet even the dogs eat the crumbs that fall from their masters' table."

Booyah! You like apples? How 'bout *them apples*!

Jesus smiled that broad, endearing smile of his. "My mother, great is your faith! May it be done for you as you wish." With that he gave her a huge hug.

"We have nothing to lose but our chains."

His disciples, confused, didn't know what had just happened. Where was the classic Jesus retort? That wit that had shut down the scribes and Pharisees (the religious and civil leaders) back in Jerusalem a couple days before? He minced no words with them, insisting that people aren't made impure by inconsequential externals; but rather, by the hurtfulness they spew toward others. Where was that guy?

"All Things New"

Jesus had the reputation of being outspoken. Oddly, he seldom spoke up at the times or in the ways listeners, even those closest to him expected.

I've always thought of this story as being about challenging prejudice, as in, "Why are you singling out the Syrians for mistreatment . . . Western conservatives?" But I have friends who insist this story is about Jesus staying true to his singular mission to the Jews and not being distracted by the many other good things he could have been doing.

The truth is that trying to peg what any story is about is like trying to nail the number of jelly beans in a mason jar. A story can be about a lot of things and nothing definitive all at the same time. We understand this intuitively about other stories, but with scripture we want to reduce every story to some eternally salient point. However, if we insist that scripture, particularly the story of

Jesus, is "the greatest story ever told in the greatest book ever written," then why should we expect that story to function by different conventions than those we find in the best literature?

This is something important to note about a COMPOST approach. COMPOSTable readings/tellings of sacred myths no longer try to boil narratives down to one all-important moral. They admit other interpretations, an important act of humility that all people of faith should adopt. This concept is so deeply embedded in Judaism and Christianity that the first two chapters of the Hebrew Bible (the Book of Genesis) offer two different versions of how and why the world came into being. They outright contradict each other, leaving us with the unmistakable impression that "Which one is right?" is of little significance to faith. COMPOSTable readings/tellings of sacred myths allow our faith stories to do the multifaceted work that they've always done—forming and informing us on multiple levels all at the same time.

> The faith of those considered closest to Jesus does not invalidate those furthest away.

Although humility constrains me from attempting to make the conclusive statement of what the story is about, the inkling I now get from this story is that the "faith" of those closest to Jesus doesn't get to invalidate those furthest away. Now don't hear me wrong. I'm not saying my faith doesn't make your faith wrong as long as we both claim Jesus as our personal Lord and Savior. I'm not even saying that your faith doesn't invalidate my faith or lack thereof if I don't claim Jesus. I'm speaking as one who claims Jesus to others who claim Jesus, saying no one is out-of-bounds, no matter what he or she claims. One's faith, however deep, doesn't get to invalidate another human being.[7]

[7] Sorry supporters of the so-called "Religious Freedom Reformation Acts" aimed at the disenfranchisement of fellow LGBTQIA citizens. Your attempts at exclusion have no merit in either places of faith or the public square.

This revelation may only matter to Christians and others who find the Jesus myth formative. Still, I know other faiths have sacred myths, teachings that hint at a very similar thing. In his interview for *On Being on NPR*, South African Archbishop Desmond Tutu speaks of this very realization as pivotal in ending "apart-ness," apartheid, in South Africa. As Krista Tippett points out in a question to Archbishop Tutu, in addition to the political diplomacy involved in enfranchising black South Africans, Tutu and other freedom fighters had to wrestle with the Dutch Reformed Church, the primary denomination in South Africa, which sanctioned and sustained apartheid almost to the very end.

Tutu replied:

> One of the wonderful things was how in fact we had
> this interfaith cooperation—Muslims, Christians, Jews,
> Hindus. And now, you know, when you hear people speak
> disparagingly about, say, Islam, and you say they've
> forgotten that that faith inspired people to great acts of
> courage.
>
> You discovered that the thing you were fighting
> against was too big for divided churches, for divided
> religious community. And each of the different faith
> communities realized some of the very significant central
> teachings about the worth of a human being, about the
> unacceptability of injustice and oppression.[8]

What a startling discovery! Imagine how much better things
would be in the world—as soon as tomorrow—if the 5.5 billion
people who claim faith simply stopped calling into question the
human and/or divine legitimacy of everybody else.

Now I know how we people of faith are. Perhaps you are trying
to convert this inkling about the inviolate validity of all into a
concept that will leave you pretty much where you've been. Feel
free, but the way stories of faith should indict us, no matter how
open and affirming we thought we were, the Jesus myth, this
story we've just shared in particular, is pushing those boundaries.

Many of us think our boundaries are just fine. Some of us believe
God personally set them. I get it—the desire to hold onto some
clear, uncompromising demarcations between right and wrong.
I know that's the language some substitute for phrases that have
fallen out of favor, phrases that may sound politically incorrect or
downright discriminatory. However, let me just offer that anything
worth holding onto can withstand the repeated scrutiny of those
who disagree.

On the other hand, unwillingness to scrutinize one's boundaries
robs one's self and those labeled "wrong" of the opportunity to
begin healing from the damage caused by placing human beings
out-of-bounds.

Tutu shares this self-indicting example of how insidiously
injuriously any boundaries are that place fellow human beings out-
of-bounds:

[8] "[Unedited] Desmond
Tutu with Krista Tippett,"
On Being with Krista
Tippett, April 29, 2010,
http://www.onbeing.org/
program/desmond-tutus-
god-surprises/85.

I think that we have very gravely underestimated the damage that apartheid inflicted on all of us. The damage to our psyches, the damage that has made. I've often told people a story that— it shocked me. I went to Nigeria when I was working for the World Council of Churches, and I was due to fly to Jos. And so I go to Lagos airport, and I get onto the plane, and the two pilots in the cockpit are both black. And [I tell you], I just grew inches. You know, it was fantastic because we had been told that blacks can't do this.

And we have a smooth takeoff and then we hit the mother and father of turbulence. I mean, it was quite awful, scary. Do you know, I can't believe it but the first thought that came to my mind was, "Hey, there's no white man in that cockpit. Are those blacks going to be able to make it?" And well of course, they obviously made it—here I am. But the thing is, I had not known that I was damaged to the extent of thinking that somehow actually what those white people who had kept drumming into us in South Africa about our being inferior, about our being incapable, it had lodged somewhere in me.[9]

[9] Ibid.

We all have our hang-ups. No amount of mental assent can rewrite a lifetime of what Edwin Markham refers to in his poem "Outwitted" as circle drawing.

He drew a circle that shut me out —

Heretic, rebel, a thing to flout.

So that's not what I'm talking about. I'm advocating, based upon the intuitions of beloved community that arise out of this story, that we finally learn to live in grace toward those we have so many hang-ups about—the one thing Jesus actually commands, the one thing Christians seldom try.

But Love and I had the wit to win:

We drew a circle that took him in![10]

[10] Edwin Markham, "Outwitted," in *The Shoes of Happiness and Other Poems* (Century, 1913), 1.

Perhaps in living graciously toward one another we will realize the answers to many of our questions. It could be we will develop the strength of relationship to ask them compassionately of the people they concern. Maybe we will be chastened about the dehumanizing nature of some of our questions and concerns. Or just possibly, we will discover that our concerns were unfounded. Who knows? Being in prolonged proximity with those who concern us so just might make us better people. It did for me.

How I Made It Over

I am a recovering fundamentalist. I was raised in a tradition known for its commitment to a "high view" of scripture. We were people of the Book (the Bible) and had interpretations that, though not thoughtlessly literal, were strictly construed. One of the things we took very seriously was discerning that which should be called sin. When your sense of eternal destiny is wrapped up in whether you get the question of sin right, you tend to take it quite seriously. So we'd read the Old and New Testament lists of thou shalts and thou shalt nots, and we sought to honor them as best we could, with no real acknowledgment of the evolution of social context. Thus I grew up with a pretty definite view of sexuality. There was stuff within bounds and stuff out-of-bounds, and regardless of individual choices to adhere to those standards, it was clear what those standards were.

It was through this lens that I experienced my classroom becoming the hangout for the LGBTQ kids at the high school where I taught. When I recalled my stepfather telling me that I would need to be open to ministering to anyone, I saw these students there as my opportunity. It wasn't until years later that I realized that those kids were ministering to me as much as I was to them. Even though I didn't get it at the time, they were teaching me about impartial love.[11]

[11] bell hooks talks about love being impartial, not unconditional. I find this description of love most compelling, particularly when talking about an appropriate response to injustice.

For several years thereafter, I held onto some concerns that I felt invalidated LGBTQ "lifestyles," not the least of which was my concern for the sexual abuse I knew that most of my LGBTQ family, friends, and associates had suffered. I shudder now at the thought, but I used to refer to them as "reactionarily gay" (please forgive me), and that, for me, was something totally different than those who claimed to have known they were gay all their lives. I was committed to parsing the difference between loving the sinner and hating the sin. I was convinced of

> What is it about us that, even when we are free to do otherwise, we structure, settle for or fight tooth-and-nail to preserve systems that legitimize some while delegitimizing others based on criteria of such little consequence?

the importance of living in grace toward others, but I was also committed to graciously "calling sin by its right name," like my former student in chapter 1.

My understanding of holding everyone's validity inviolate didn't come overnight. It was a process facilitated by ongoing conversations with lots of different people, particularly those I was hung up about. As I learned to appreciate my LGBTQIA students keeping up with me even after they graduated. As I was reminded of my cousin Cassandra who died in 1982. Although abused as a child, she was far from tragically transsexual. As I encountered LGBTQIA colleagues who had the same, if not greater, hopes for their students as I and had friends who questioned my commitments to such narrow theological certainties. As I witnessed from afar the transformation of a guy I worked with at summer camp who obviously had internalized a great deal of stress trying to keep his secret, which manifested physically as runaway acne and social awkwardness. I ran into him years later, and he was looking and feeling fabulous after he had come to love himself for who he is. As I watched my cousin-in-law Krystal courageously come out amidst the fundamentalist stronghold in which she was raised and I awakened to the agony of friends still closeted. Eventually, I recognized the hurtfulness in which I was complicit and decided I, for one, need not be a part of it any more.

Who knew? "It gets better,"[12] even for supposedly well-meaning religious know-it-alls like myself.[13]

A Political Reality

Have you ever noticed how you get to know some people quickly? That is a norm for me. More often than not, given a little one-on-one time, folks will share with me intimate details about themselves that it takes years for them to divulge with others. I genuinely like people, which perhaps they sense, and have a short memory, so folks don't have to worry that what they've shared will be thrown back in their faces. Still, every so often I'll meet someone not so easy to know, which intrigues me. Particularly when it is clear we both like each other. That is the nature of my friendship with Jacob Kuntz. Whereas I obscure a lot in all I might say, Jacob is naturally reserved, but we can both flip the switch to silly and get a laugh pretty easily, leaving few the wiser that we haven't necessarily opened up.

One of the things Jacob does in opening up is write and share music. Not only can he turn a phrase, but it's full of oft missing perspective. One such song, "Last Message," he shared in the

[12] "It Gets Better Project" is a very important campaign targeted at engendering hope and reducing suicide rates among LGBTQIA young people.

[13] To chart the path of similar conversions, check out the stories of Carlton Pearson, pastor, singer, and author, and David Blankenhorn, founder of the Institute for American Values.

cold of January 2012 while a group of us served Communion to one another at the close of a planning retreat for the annual Wild Goose Festival. Immediately, the lyric opened my ears to what was missing from the conversation about being open and affirming of routinely marginalized groups of people:

And on the third day I put on my best

I went to the place where they laid him to rest

When I arrived he'd already gone

Singing, "This love's for everyone!"

Mary his favorite took me aside

And told me the scene that had passed before her eyes

He showed them his hands and they begged him to speak

And he said, "This love's for everyone!"

Peter said, "Lord, are you out of your mind?

"The same love for your servants and the vain Pharisees?"

But Jesus said, "Brother, did you miss everything?

"This love's for everyone!"

And in the garden I was playing guitar

And through the trees I heard him crying to God

When I awoke he had already gone

Saying,"This love's for everyone!"

I heard he went singing, "This love's for everyone!"

In my last year on local public television, I missed an opportunity to interview Archbishop Desmond Tutu because of a last minute change in his schedule. Although I regret not being able to sit with him, truth is, my wife is right: I wasn't ready then to have the conversation I would like to be able to look back upon. But as I heard him speak recently, I was reminded of why I yearn for the opportunity to sit at the feet of elders such as Tutu—to be reminded of the grandness of their vision, to counter in me the narrowing of perspective that seems to afflict many in leadership today.

Tutu reflected,

> We didn't struggle in order just to change the complexion of those who sit in the Union Buildings—the Union Buildings are something like your capitol and so on. It wasn't to change the complexion, it was to change the quality of our community. . . . We wanted to see a society that was a compassionate society, a caring society, a society where you might not necessarily be madly rich but you knew that you counted.[14]

In a world that has initiated enough violence based on the perceived invalidity of others to last all of our lifetimes, how could we not want the better society of which Tutu dreams?

[14] "[Unedited] Desmond Tutu with Krista Tippett," On Being with Krista Tippett, April 29, 2010, http://www.onbeing.org/program/desmond-tutus-god-surprises/85.

CHAPTER THREE

Suspicions Concerning Other People's Stories

A literary agent once told me I should be more emotive on paper, as I am in person. He was right. Nonetheless, I'm not sure that how I feel about the stuff I write about is printable, but I'll give it a try.

I HATE with a passion *The Help* and all stories like it. Yes, that "winning," "graceful and real," "VERY courageous," "masterfully plotted novel," "full of heart and history." The "good old-fashioned," "magical novel" that is a "pitch-perfect depiction" that "strikes every note with authenticity" and "attention to historical detail, dialect, and characterization."[1]

The fact that the National Academy of Motion Picture Arts and Sciences nominated the movie adaptation of the novel for four Oscars in 2012 gives me reason to hate it all the more.[2]

My initial disdain for Kathryn Stockett's story came just prior to its book club craze as my wife read it and shared with me troublesome portions of the narrative. I would shake my head and ask, "What else would you expect from someone trying to tell someone else's story?" Don't get me wrong. Stockett can string words together as well as the next person. In fact, as I read—I admit I could not subject myself to the novel word for word in its entirety—I could see Stockett trying hard. However, certain words just don't ring true in the mouths of black characters, and certain thoughts, I know from cultural experience, would have led to different conclusions.

I'm sure Stockett meant no harm, but I couldn't make sense of why in a post-colonial world she would even dare address the story at all. Why not tell the story exclusively through the

[1] Praises offered by Susan Larson (*Times-Picayune*), Karen Valby (*Entertainment Weekly*), Marian Keyes (*The Brightest Star in the Sky*), Heller McAlpin (*Christian Science Monitor*), *Publishers Weekly* (Louisa Ermelino, reviews director), *New York Daily News*, Robert Hicks (*The Widow of the South*), Carol Memmott (*USA Today*), Sybil Steinberg (*Washington Post*) and Sarah Sacha Dollacker (*Atlanta Journal-Constitution*) respectively—none of whom look like the presumptive main characters.

[2] It was nominated for more than one hundred prestigious awards.

eyes of Skeeter, the fictionalized version of Stockett, and overtly acknowledge the limitations of her own perspective, like Sue Monk Kidd in *The Secret Life of Bees* or Barbara Kingsolver in *The Poisonwood Bible*? What chance did Stockett think she had of ever approaching the emotional, intellectual, spiritual, or social insight into the black experience of a Toni Morrison, Alice Walker, or Lawrence Hill, all of whom have written about similar characters in similar situations? The book may have had a significant number of black characters, but obviously it was not about black people, and white people made Stockett a millionaire several times over for telling them a story about themselves they wanted to hear.

My favorite review of *The Help*, "Chocolate Breast Milk," was written by creative writing professor and author Honorée Fanonne Jeffers on her blog *Wheatley Remastered*.[3] With easy, incisive prose Jeffers articulates what she resents as "tone-deaf depictions" in both the book and the movie. "We never see the personal lives of the black women who work as 'the help.' Almost every time they appear on screen, they are either tending to White others, or they are talking about White others' goings on. To see this movie, one would think that these Black women had no other concerns than the Whites they work for." They are the quintessential "magic" Negroes. Even in the book, Jeffers points out, "85–90% of [the black ladies'] internal dialogues surround their White employers; they are preoccupied with 'their' White folks. The White heroine, however, has a rich internal dialogue that takes her away from the Black women constantly."

That last point was the one Jeffers found most disturbing, and for good reason. However, the critique that has haunted me since reading it is the one she gives about this particular scene of the story:

> [The one time a character, Minny,] decides to act alone on her rage, she does so in a way that is (to me) morally transgressive; when her employer fires her, she bakes a pie using her own feces as an ingredient and feeds it to the woman in retaliation. As I sat there in the audience and listened to the guffaws of the White moviegoers at the "feces pie" scene, I could only think, what has become of a woman who gathers her body waste in her actual hands and cooks with it, in her *own* kitchen? Where were her

[3] http://phillisremastered.wordpress.com/2011/08/11/chocolate-breast-milk-a-review-of-the-help/.

children while she was stirring up feces? How can she or her home ever be *clean* again? For me, it was not the humorous, empowering moment it was intended to be [à la the car burning scene in *Waiting to Exhale*], but rather tragic and pathetic. It made me want to weep for Minnie [*sic*].

When harm has been done over the long term, you can't just skip to the good part

I couldn't ask for a more graphic example of what I find so deeply problematic about Stockett and movie director Tate Taylor presuming to tell a story that is not heritably their own. Beyond the tragic literary irony and real life hypocrisy of Stockett rooting her narrative in the lived experience of a woman named Ablene Cooper (Stockett's brother's nanny), is the fact that she refused to pay Ablene (Aibileen in the book) for the use of her story.[4] When Stockett finally gets to the fiction part of her storyline, because of her lack of cultivated affinity with the domestics whose story she tells, she attributes to these black women behavior that is so bizarre and other than herself so as to make it utterly, immutably inferior.

Non-black people then consume Stockett and Taylor's fiction—I mean devour it, over five million copies of the book sold, a *New York Times* bestseller for more than one hundred weeks running, a movie adaptation with box office receipts of more than $200 million, all within its first three years—and walk away thinking they know something more or better about black folks.

Not convinced? Let me illustrate for you the devastating potency of this way of cannibalizing others. Consider the intractable myth that blacks were/are less evolved, more animal-like humanoids than whites.[5] It's convenient to forget that this was considered a valid field of study in some anthropological and biological circles as recently as mid-twentieth century. Doctors of this-and-that used to talk about how the slope of the forehead and the set of the eyes and the flatness of the nose were all indicative of lesser intelligence and more criminality. To this end, Black Sambo, the happy-go-lucky monkey-man, illustrations of who was taking over Washington and local governments in the latter 1800s helped to bring an end to gains made by blacks during the First Reconstruction and to anchor the South in a kind of precognitive rationalization of Jim Crow.[6]

[4] Meaning no harm isn't the same as doing no harm; neither is meaning no harm the same as doing good. http://abcnews.go.com/Health/lawsuit-black-maid-ablene-cooper-sues-author-kathryn/story?id=12968562

[5] Though neither knows how to cook, apes have been known to throw their feces, and dogs will eat theirs.

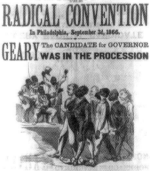

1866 flyer calling black political participation "radical." Replace the black figures with visually stereotypical Muslims, immigrants, queer folk or a woman running for president, and it sounds like 2016.

[6] As Melissa Harris-Perry points out in her magnificent work of applied political science,

The Freedman's Bureau (founded two whole years after emancipation) was an early US attempt at welfare expansion beyond white people. One can't remain credible making the same specious argument for 150 years, all the while claiming this time it's finally applicable.

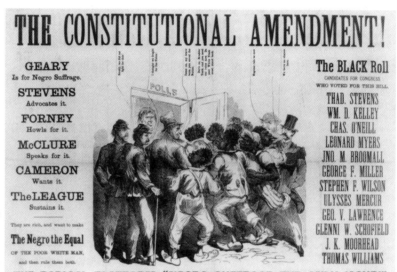

In 1866, "Negro suffrage" was code for "race traitor." According to this, only an unpatriotic suffrage advocate ("race traitor," "radical Islam sympathizer," "pro-amnesty," "queer-lover") would vote for the 13th, 14th or 15th Amendments.

Child's play. Sambo book images (1908). The indoctrination–i.e., justification–starts young.

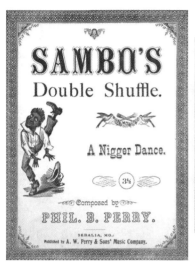

Child's play.
[Left] Sambo
sheet music
(1883). [Right] A
1909 poor white
boys' first-grade
classroom,
complete with
Sambo mural in
the background.

Child's play.
A 1924 Sambo
board game.

Sister Citizen (Yale Univ. Press, 2011), black women were saddled with an even more complex set of mythic stereotypes that aid(ed) in the rationalization of white supremacy—from slavery's hypersexual Jezebel to The Help's asexual Mammy. "The idea of black women's sexual wantonness was important to late nineteenth- and early twentieth-century nation-building efforts. Race and gender science informed public ideas of who was capable of citizenship as the country reestablished the basis of political participation following the Civil War. Science and its growing hegemony of knowledge underlay the nineteenth-century's racial ideology and iconography. . . . The treatment of Saartjie Baartman, the so-called Hottentot Venus, is an iconic example of how black women's bodies became central to the process of arraying human beings in ascending order from apelike to human, African to European, black to white, female to male, savage to civilized. Baartman was a Khoikhoi woman from South Africa who became a canonized exhibit of London's Piccadilly Circus as a result of her supposedly abnormal sexual organs. . . . Baartman's genitalia and buttocks served as observable scientific evidence that black women were not fully civilized. Science was used to underscore the

But I don't have to reach back before birth for instances of this type of thinking playing out. When I was six years old, my school, operated by my church, closed. The closure was a shame precipitated in part by a board discussion in which a white church elder, a physician and father of three beautiful daughters, expressed concern in light of the supposed "scientific fact" that black boys (of which there had been a recent influx) sexually mature early.[7] I remember Jimmy the Greek, then a famous sportscaster, a few years later was fired for tripping over himself trying to make the observation that blacks appear to be evolutionarily gifted (bred) for running. Oh, but it didn't stop there. Before I could get out of the '80s I found myself taking sides in a potential school fight[8] because a white classmate got a little too liberal with his commentary on how the African exchange student played basketball like an ape. Yes, and lest we forget, there was all that talk back then about hip-hop sounding like "jungle music."

Thank goodness I was spared many more of these experiences because I matriculated at an historically black high school and college—although my college did have a music department chair who insisted the beat and bass of popular black music overly excited the "lower passions." After college I learned adults tend to be a little more covert about their denigration. But wasn't it just the other day (29 February 2012) that a sitting U.S. Federal Judge disseminated a "private... joke" about President Obama, suggesting Obama's mother slept with a dog on the same night he was conceived.[9]

As one who grew up with access to the benefits of a middle-class education and existence, I know that those who invested in me hoped to remove me from this type of thinking and being in the world, yet somehow, someway this nonsense keeps finding its way back into my present! It keeps being re-introduced to each new generation in movies and TV shows and music and news coverage and political discourse and the unchecked slaughtering of people of color in the middle of the street. And as easy as it is to want to think otherwise, this shit is not just happening on the fringe, which suggests that, if we know nothing else, we need to be assured of the abiding negative effects of projecting our worst imaginations on or otherwise speaking with authority into the experiences of those we haven't taken time to know.

Returning to Jeffers's review of The Help, she concludes with the following, which I find quite revelatory:

At the very beginning of [the movie] *The Help*, Skeeter (the white aspiring writer telling the black domestics' story) poses the question to Aibileen, "How did you feel, leaving your own child while you took care of other people's children?"

That question is never answered.

Aibileen's son's life isn't explored, even in flashback; she only talks briefly about the horrible way in which he died. In the movie, we only see his picture. It is as if his only contribution to the movie is to provide motivation for Aibileen's later actions, after he's dead. Her mother's love, her mother's grief, is condensed into 2 or 3 minutes. And in reality, she doesn't claim her own voice—as a mother, as a woman, or someone who has her own inner mystery. She has no voice unless someone White is in the room.

The only voice given to black people in *The Help* is that of a privileged white woman raised with black domestic help who could not begin to understand their journey or their plight. My disdain for Stockett's story is rooted in its lack of authenticity and her unmitigated gall. I am appalled by her unbounded efforts to co-opt another's story.[10]

Mythic Proportions

The European colonial project of the eighteenth, nineteenth, and twentieth centuries even in its most benevolent forms was embedded in the myth of being the keeper of someone else's destiny, someone else's story. Rudyard Kipling called it "The White Man's Burden:"

Take up the White Man's burden—

Send forth the best ye breed—

Go, bind your sons to exile

To serve your captives' need;

To wait, in heavy harness,

On fluttered folk and wild—

Your new-caught sullen peoples,

Half devil and half child.

ideological biases of racist, misogynist America, and black women's vulnerability was codified in law. The myth of black women's unrestrained sexuality operated in both slavery and freedom as a means of justifying racial and gender exploitation."

[7] Don't miss the implication.

[8] Yes, we had those at my little Christian private school.

[9] And, mind you, that's not the only, just the politest interpretation I can think of.

[10] For a more detailed accounting and analysis of manifestations of this historic "white rage," see Carol Anderson's *White Rage: The Unspoken Truth of Our Racial Divide* (Bloomsbury, 2016).

[11] Not everyone did, of course, but it would be a mistake to believe that "justice for all" has ever been a majority opinion in the West.

[12] John Flint, *Cecil Rhodes* (Boston: Little, Brown and Company, 1974), 248–50.

[13] Chinua Achebe, *Things Fall Apart* (Anchor Books, 1994).

[14] "Dominion" as described in the Hebrew creation stories has nothing to do with the European notion of divine right. It had to do with what might be described as a divine responsibility to care for or take care of, what one might describe as "stewardship," like that demonstrated by the Maasai in caring for cattle. The passage quoted previously would be better understood,

Persons of European descent around the world were encouraged to believe in Europe's "divine right" to colonize as much of the world as it could—even others' minds and cultures.[11] "Poverty is better under [the British] flag," Cecil Rhodes (after whom the Rhodes Scholarship is named) declared, "than wealth under a foreign one."[12]

Colonizers often justified and advanced their endeavors with the Bible, as Chinua Achebe so masterfully documents in *Things Fall Apart*.[13] The colonially interpreted biblical synonym for the myth of divine right is "dominion." The sentiment upon which it is based is first found in Genesis 1: "Then God said, 'Let us make humankind in our image, according to our likeness; and let them have dominion over the fish of the sea, and over the birds of the air, and over the cattle, and over all the wild animals of the earth, and over every creeping thing that creeps upon the earth.'"

This misunderstanding of dominion gets demonstrated throughout scripture, most notably in Israel's sense of divine right to conquer Canaan following their exodus from Egypt. European nations used Israel's example as carte blanche to subjugate any group of people that organized according to a different set of sacred myths.[14]

The fact that European certainties regarding "dominion" involved a literalistic, misguided, absurd reading of Hebrew scripture is not what makes it myth. Again, "myth" is not synonym for "falsehood." What makes it a myth is that most of the modern world has been physically, intellectually, and emotionally organized around the notion of such dominance.

In the West, there are almost too many examples to know where to start. From the way banks and old-wealth corporations were set up and currently operate, to the way federal, state, and local governments and other societal institutions are organized to function, Western powers exerting their will is inevitably excused as being right, reasonable, or otherwise unavoidable.

Under the umbrella of dominion, the United States has broken every treaty it ever made with the First Nations,[15] resulting in the death or perpetual poverty of millions of Native Americans, with limited hope for justice. Yet we wax nostalgic about our noble ancestors' good-faith efforts to civilize this land, as if it previously had been unoccupied and unused. Beyond our interaction with First Nations, according to Stephen Kinzer,[16] the United States has admitted (operative word) to executing various regime changes fourteen times in its nearly 240 years of existence (none of them successful in securing the long-term ally we sought). Nevertheless, we hold to the view of ourselves as a non-imperial power, even though our own old history texts and nineteenth-century public figures used the language of imperialism with pride to describe our endeavors in Mexico, Philippines, Hawaii, Puerto Rico, and other territories.

Maintaining the myth of dominion means that our systems and structures are woefully inadequate to meet the rapid changes taking place in the twenty-first century. Sticking to inadequate ways of doing things may be because we've failed to engage imagination to do things differently. Or it may be our resistance to letting go of the de facto privilege our myths allow. In an increasingly global society, there are still those whose stories have currency only when told through the filter of their former (and recurrent) colonizers.

> "Then God said, 'Let us make humankind in our image, according to our likeness; and let them [take responsibility for] the fish of the sea, and the birds of the air. . . . " Author and activist Lisa Sharon Harper does some good work with the notion of dominion in her new book *The Very Good Gospel* (Colorado Springs: WaterBrook, 2016).

> **Special Snowflake Syndrome:**
> "Each snowflake in an avalanche pleads not guilty."
> ~Stanislaw Jerzy Lec, as characterized by Son of Baldwin

Better Than You Know Yourself

This reminds me of a story about the ancient nation of Israel after Babylonian and Persian exile. Cyrus, Darius, and Artaxerxes, kings of the Medeo-Persian Empire had, on separate occasions, commissioned Ezra and Nehemiah, Israelite captives who worked in the royal courts, to lead a confederacy of expatriates back to the Israelite homeland to reestablish themselves.

With the completion of the wall around Jerusalem, Israel's capital city, a wave of national pride arose. It had only taken fifty-two days of focused effort. The repatriated exiles, returned from Babylon, were excited about being recognizable as a nation again, no longer the conquered and displaced people whose gentry had been carried off into bondage and whose peasants had been left behind to eke out subsistence on the surrounding lands. And as is often the case, as the returning gentry felt better about themselves, they also felt better about how God felt about them. The possibility of God's renewed pride for Israel was exhilarating. Had God not already extended divine favor by allowing them to return and restore the temple and the city walls?

[15] Courey Toensing, Gale "'Honor Treaties': Human Rights Chiefs Message," *Indian Country Today Media Network* (web), August 23, 2013.

[16] Stephen, Kinzer, *Overthrow: America's Century of Regime Change from Hawaii to Iraq* (Times Books, 2006). You can find an hour lecture overview of the book on C-SPAN, given by Stephen Kinser at Northwestern University, April 10, 2006, http://www.c-span.org/video/?c4499417/stephen-kinzer-talks-book-overthrow-americas-century-regime-change-hawaii-iraq.

Though the total city had not been rebuilt, the three most important symbols of a promising future were reestablished. First, the Temple, a symbol of God's abiding presence. Now the walls and gates. Walls and gates are symbols of a nation's self-determination. Gates and walls also give a nation the ability to protect itself as necessary. And wasn't that what God wanted? Wasn't that why God had allowed them to return: to redefine themselves and to protect that renewed vision?

Right or wrong, that is exactly what Nehemiah, former cup-bearer to the king of Persia, appointed governor of Israel, and Ezra, former scribe to the king of Persia commissioned as high priest, believed. Once the physical walls that defined Israel as a nation were rebuilt, these two men believed it was time to erect by analogy the cultural walls that would help define the restored Israel further. After seventy years in exile, who were they? They were the people of God's favor, were they not?

What does God favor?

This is a tough question to answer because people do not always see divine favor as the same thing in every instance. It's not that scripture doesn't offer definite clues. However, there is always the temptation to trick ourselves into believing that God is in favor of whatever we favor at any particular time.

> "We must . . . raise questions of the author [or storyteller] about his or her assumptions about the world and people's relationship to one another."
> ~Renita Weems, womanist scholar

Our understanding of God seldom exceeds the limits of our own perspective. Imagine a time when we and our thinking were far less global. (Right, yesterday.) If I were looking at a map, appreciating the particular topographic features of my own country, it would be very easy for me to assume that since the land I love is a certain way, surely other countries that I can't see from my vantage point must be quite similar. I may wonder, "If God saw fit to shape my native land in certain ways—to give it certain features and certain natural resources (a certain form of government or a certain religious heritage)—isn't that a sign of what God favors? Isn't that what all lands God favors look like?"

But just looking at my own country on my map, I can't see what other countries look like on the other side of the world. My appreciation for the many different lands or people or languages or food or clothes or art or faith or politics, and so on is limited by the little I can see. This is true of anyone.

Nehemiah and Ezra were limited by what they could see. One such limitation was their preoccupation with respectability. They were respectable people multiple times over. Both had been officials in the court of the most powerful king in that part of the world, which gave them a great deal of personal respectability. Both men were descendants of a long line of respectable Israelites, cultural heroes and heroines immortalized in Israel's stories. To add to that, their families possessed land, title, and position in Jewish society that, if they were successful in reestablishing the pre-exile social order, they would be able to reclaim.

These were the ways they defined respectability: position, possession, parentage. They had grown up in Babylon seeing this type of respectability rewarded and had learned to value it. So, naturally, when they opened the book of Moses (Torah) to glean how their forebears had interpreted God's favor, what stood out to them sounded like God's shared preoccupation with this same type of respectability.

When they heard, "It is from the nations around you that you may acquire male and female slaves. You may also acquire them from among the aliens residing with you, and from their families that are with you, who have been born in your land; and they may be your property. You may keep them as a possession for your children after you, for them to inherit as property. These you may treat as slaves, but as for your fellow Israelites, no one shall rule over the other with harshness."[17] They took it to mean, "God favors Jews, not Gentiles." But they missed, "The alien who resides with you shall be to you as the citizen among you; you shall love the alien [stranger, foreigner, gentile] as yourself, for you were aliens in the land of Egypt."[18]

[17] Leviticus 25:44-46.

[18] Leviticus 19:34.

And when they read, "The LORD will make you abound in prosperity, in the fruit of your womb, in the fruit of your livestock, and in the fruit of your ground in the land that the LORD swore to your ancestors to give you . . . if you obey the commandments of the LORD your God . . . But if you will not obey the LORD your God . . . cursed shall be the fruit of your womb, the fruit of your ground, the increase of your cattle, and the issue of your flock."[19] They thought they read "God favors the wealthy," or "wealth is a sign of God's favor." But they missed: "Since there will never cease to be some in need on the earth, I therefore command you, 'Open your hand to the poor and needy neighbor in your land. . . . Be careful that you do not entertain a mean thought . . . and give

[19] Deuteronomy 28:11,13,15,18.

[20] Deuteronomy 15:11; Deuteronomy 15:9.

nothing; your neighbor might cry to the LORD against you, and you would incur guilt."[20]

They read, "The equivalent for a male . . . twenty to sixty years of age . . . shall be fifty shekels of silver. . . . If the person is a female, the equivalent is thirty shekels."[21] They thought they read "God favors men over women." And maybe they did read that. Maybe some of their ancestors shared the same limitations and preoccupations as had Ezra and Nehemiah.

[21] Leviticus 27: 2–5.

To celebrate the completion of the physical walls and to communicate the need for the building of an analogous wall of respectability, Nehemiah and Ezra called the people of Israel together—at least all they believed could understand the message they wanted to communicate—and read to them out of the Torah. Once they were finished reading, Nehemiah and Ezra commissioned the Levites to lead small group discussions of the value of respectability and how they as a people might achieve it and earn God's favor. When all was done, the people present began to weep with guilt. They obviously figured they had done some things wrong. If nothing else, they had not been as respectable as they were now hearing they should be.

With all sincerity, these elite of Israel began to look for ways to become more respectable (and retain God's favor). The first thing they thought they could do was to start observing the cultural holidays and feasts that had been forgotten while in exile. It was great! They began to make all sorts of promises regarding things they would do or remember. Good things. Just things. Particularly, ways of demonstrating the Sabbath ethic of enough: appreciating God's provision by resting from work each week; giving the land time to rest every seven years; forgiving debts; routine sharing of their harvest with those in need (those without and those in vocation); participating in the rhythmic communal practices that remind one of this type of justice. Good things. Just things.

But then came a practice that seemed out of place, off-key. The ever more respectable Israelite elites found written from the book of Moses "that no Ammonite or Moabite should ever enter the assembly of God, because [years ago] they did not . . . [help] the Israelites with bread and water, but hired Balaam against them to curse them—yet . . . God turned the curse into a blessing. When the people heard the Law, they separated from Israel all those of foreign descent."[22] How odd, how random, to embrace a one thousand-year-old grudge as if unto the Lord.

[22] Nehemiah 13: 1–3.

Nehemiah went as far as to record:

> In those days also I saw Jews who had married women of Ashdod, Ammon, and Moab; and half of their children spoke the language of Ashdod, and they could not speak the language of Judah, but spoke the language of various peoples. And I contended with them and cursed them and beat some of them and pulled out their hair! And I made them take an oath in the name of God, saying, "You shall not give your daughters to their sons, or take their daughters for your sons or for yourselves. . . ."

> And one of the sons of Jehoiada, son of the high priest Eliashib, was the son-in-law of Sanballat the Horonite; I chased him away from me. Remember them, O my God, because they have defiled the priesthood, the covenant of the priests and the Levites.

> Thus I cleansed them from everything foreign. . . . Remember me, O my God, for good.[23]

[23] Nehemiah 13:23–26; 28–31.

How did the respectable Nehemiah and his fellow elites of Israelite society move to assault people and ask God to bless it?

One would think that the vehement exclusion of one group—foreigners—for the sake of increased respectability would be enough, but to do it once is to become addicted. It didn't take long before the respectable Israelite insiders had compiled a growing list of outsiders to pick on: foreigners, Israelites married to people of foreign descent, the children of mixed marriages had to go (all of whom, conveniently, were longtime residents of the land these returnees from Babylon were trying to reclaim). Those without land—women, children born out of wedlock, eunuchs (the sexually marginalized)—weren't banished; but rather, were afforded few or no political rights. Only the most respectable could have full rights in the Temple assembly—only they could retain God's favor. At least that's what Nehemiah, Ezra, and those most like them had come to believe. That's the story they tell in the books that bear their names in the Hebrew Bible. They were certain in their standing and had a lot of disparaging things to say about those clearly outside of God's favor.

Given the chance, I'm sure those marginalized would have had a different story to tell about Nehemiah and Ezra's return from exile. In fact, they did, as a part of what was left of the tradition of the

school of the prophets from Elijah and Elisha's time. Their protests now make up the third movement of the book of Isaiah in the Bible. In the great tradition of Isaiah, their teacher, who had stood boldly against the excesses of Israel's leaders before seeing them carried off into Babylonian captivity, these students now spoke out with poetic potency against the excesses of the ever so respectable elite who had returned from Babylon:

Thus says the Lord:

Maintain justice, and do what is right,

for soon my salvation will come,

and my deliverance be revealed.

Happy is the mortal who does this,

the one who holds it fast,

who keeps the sabbath, not profaning it,

and refrains from doing any evil.

Do not let the foreigner joined to the Lord say,

"The Lord will surely separate me from his people;"

and do not let the eunuch say,

"I am just a dry tree."[24]

For thus says the Lord:

To the eunuchs who keep my sabbaths,

who choose the things that please me

and hold fast my covenant,

I will give, in my house and within my walls,

a monument[25] *and a name*

better than sons and daughters;

[24] Some eunuchs were such because they lacked sexual desire due to loss or asexuality. In reference to loss, this is a rather, dare I say, *potent* image.

[25] Think obelisk; the Hebrew word used here is a pun for "penis," which a eunuch who had been castrated would have lost. These are arousing promises to say the least.

I will give them an everlasting name

that shall not be cut off.[26]

[26] Again, incisive imagery.

And the foreigners who join themselves to the Lord,

to minister to him, to love the name of the Lord,

and to be his servants,

all who keep the sabbath, and do not profane it,

and hold fast my covenant—

these I will bring to my holy mountain,

and make them joyful in my house of prayer;

their burnt-offerings and their sacrifices

will be accepted on my altar;

for my house shall be called a house of prayer

for all peoples.

Thus says the Lord God,

who gathers the outcasts of Israel,

I will gather others to them

besides those already gathered.[27]

[27] Isaiah 56:1-8 NRSV

It was a gracious yet pointed rebuke. These disciple prophets, who are commonly referred to among scholars as Third Isaiah, proclaimed their message in the streets of Jerusalem and throughout the Palestinian countryside. They also wrote it down, allowing the scribal and priestly classes to refer back to it.

They start by acknowledging how just Ezra and Nehemiah's initial reforms, the Sabbath reforms, were. In doing so, they save us from the temptation of labeling those we disagree with as evil. Third Isaiah also makes it clear that what God favors is justice, not cultural respectability—justice being defined as keeping Sabbath and turning away from evil. By emphasizing Sabbath practice, the students of Isaiah are appealing to the heart of the Jewish ethical tradition. To keep Sabbath is to return thanks to God, but not in word alone. It involves making sure everyone has enough and that no one has too much. In so doing, one celebrates God's

[28] Exodus 16:16–19

[29] Deuteronomy 15

[30] Exodus 23:10–12

provision by keeping it circulating throughout the community rather than concentrating with one indifidual or one family.[28] Sabbath also involves weeding out poverty wherever it takes root by periodically releasing those struggling under a load of debt[29] and by allowing the poor to glean the fields of the wealthy free of charge.[30] At length, Sabbath is a refusal to allow a system of exploitation to become the norm by putting parameters on work, accumulation, privilege, and power.

When deeply embraced, Sabbath practice eventually subverts any prejudices one may secretly harbor. So as for this business of excluding "outsiders" from God's favor, Third Isaiah sees it ultimately incongruent with a Sabbath ethic. "Let not the foreigner say . . . Let not the eunuch say . . . For this is what God

[31] Isaiah 56:3–5

says!"[31] And God's promises are so inclusive, so embracing, so opposite the exclusion that the ever more respectable elites of Israel had drifted toward. Whereas the respectable kept drawing smaller and smaller circles of who were really in God's favor, Third Isaiah paints a picture of a God who keeps redrawing the circles wider and wider so that they could eventually include you and me. How beautiful is that?

Third Isaiah's message from God excited some and dismayed others. The people debated it for a while, but Third Isaiah's vision of a radically inclusive Israel was rejected by the ever more respectable who finally reestablished political control over Israel. These gentry who had returned from Babylon eventually pushed the peasants and foreigners off the most fertile land. They allowed the gap between the rich and the poor to mount. They excluded all but those who were most like themselves from having a public voice in the future of the nation, etching more indelibly into the story of Israel this theme of "divine right." And how much favor did their pursuit of respectability curry with God? Never again in the biblical narrative is Israel completely free of some type of foreign occupation.

And what, you may wonder, happened to the rejected message of Third Isaiah? Four and a half centuries later, a young carpenter named Jesus walks into a synaogue in his hometown Nazareth to preach his first public sermon. Of all the scrolls he could have chosen, he reaches for the words of the Third Isaiah protests, dusts them off, and begins to read. He concludes, "Today this scripture has been fulfilled in your hearing," and the struggle for inclusive justice, against an exclusive respectability, is born anew!Though conveniently overlooked, Jesus stakes his enitre ministry on the vision of a just world championed by Third Isaiah—bookending his public life by claiming the words' core message as his own manifesto in the beginning at the synagogue in Nazareth and quoting from them again at the culmination of his struggle with the Exras and Nehemiahs of his day at the Temple in Jerusalem. In the midst of his dramatic "cleansing" of the Temple courtyard, Jesus quotes directly from Third Isaiah's first poem of proest against Israel's elites: "My house shall be called a house of prayer for all peoples."[32]

It's Just Easier to Forget

This is far from the traditional telling of this story; however, it is a telling that both tracks with scripture and moves us in the direction of beloved community and beyond. As one who grew up with these stories, I know that people of the Christian tradition have a great affinity for Ezra's and Nehemiah's tellings of the story. In my more than thirty years of leaning quite heavily into the stories of my tradition, I have only read one telling of Third Isaiah's protest— that of public theologian Ched Myers[33] upon whose sermon my telling of the story is based. By contrast, I have heard or read tens, maybe even hundreds, of stories in favor of Nehemiah's and Ezra's campaigns of social and political marginalization. But like Gordon Hirabayashi—perhaps an unfamiliar name—whose refusal to report to internment during World War II, originally ruled sedition by the Supreme Court,[34] was vindicated when the Supreme Court finally reversed itself. So, too, the protests of the school of Third Isaiah found themselves vindicated when a humble carpenter from Nazareth returned home and claimed this passage as the manifesto for his proto-political campaign.

Ezra and Nehemiah got it wrong, which is huge when you think about it. These are major heroes of the Judeo-Christian tradition. What's of greatest interest to me, however, is why they got it wrong. Respectability, and the pursuit thereof, is not a bad thing.[35] So where did they go wrong?

For insight into that I look to Harvard professor Marshall Ganz, whose theories of social action were at the heart of Barack Obama's successful insurgent campaign against presumptive Democratic presidential nominee Hillary Clinton in 2008. In short, Ganz's theories suggest that people are motivated to act by a progression of stories that ignite their deepest convictions. That progression, as described by Ganz, is "the story of me," "the

[32] Isaiah 56:7

[33] Ched Myers, "Biblical Interpretation as Political Practice." In J. Nowers and N. Medina, eds., Theology and the Crisis of Engagement: Essays in Honor of Lee Cormie. (Eugene:Pickwick Publications, 2013), 10-16.

[34] Read more at http://www.npr.org/blogs/thetwo-way/2012/01/04/144684260/gordon-hirabayashi-has-died-he-refused-to-go-to-wwii-internment-camp.

[35] I reassess this conclusion in chapter 8.

story of us," "the story of now." Then Senator Obama effectively told these three stories over and over as it catapulted him to "Leader of the Free World."

Not long after Obama's election, a very successful, very old, counter-narrative, that doesn't fit into either of Ganz's three categories, began to reemerge stronger than ever. The evidence of the counter-narrative's success can be found in the sales figures for Sarah Palin's book, the participation in Glenn Beck's march on Washington, the rise of the Tea Party, and the presidential candidacy of Donald Trump. If I were to name the counter-narrative after the pattern established by Ganz, I would call it "The Tale of Them." It is an attempt to tell a story that is not one's own, to attribute motives and values and worth to the experiences and actions of another.

The Tale of Them

"The tale of them" is as old as gossip, which in politics gets redefined into the more socially acceptable language of "opposition research."

"The tale of them" isn't just told on the trail to public office. Once in office, male legislators debate and pass unlimited proscriptions on female reproductive autonomy ("the tale of them"), considering turnabout foul play when legislation around male reproductive prerogative is brought up by female legislators.

In our foreign policy, the United States always has such grave concerns about sham elections elsewhere ("the tale of them") even though we continue to have difficulties of our own allowing everyone to exercise their constitutional franchise. And in diplomacy, can the stories we tell ourselves about what others might do with nuclear capability ("the tale of them") be characterized as anything but paranoid schizophrenia, considering we are the only nation in history to intentionally detonate a nuclear bomb on other human beings? Might I suggest the only reason we aren't paralyzed under the weight of our own hypocrisy is because "the tale of them" makes hypocrisy perfectly reasonable in light of the imagined threat perpetually posed by those different from us.

Spinning "the tale of them" is so problematic when described this way, but we do it all the time. And here is where I would suggest Ezra and Nehemiah went awry. When you read the books of Ezra and Nehemiah you will see that both do a bang-up job of articulating the "stories of me, us, and now," but then they get all off into "the tale of them" in such a way that once they start down the path, marginalizing any and everyone unlike themselves is a near certainty. Whether one intends it or not, "the tale of them" takes over, and it's such an easy story to tell because, like any fiction, it doesn't have to be based in actuality.

You may be asking, "What about all that talk about myth being about truth, not about fact?" Sure, when it's a myth about you, us, and now. But any myth about "the other," would be immediately suspect. For one thing, there is too much to gain by telling another's story with bias. That is not to suggest that everyone is knowingly or intentionally biased when speaking of others. Still, it doesn't cost us anything when we are, which may make us a little less careful in the telling. For another thing, social science has proven that we believe those with whom we identify more than we believe those whom we've disparaged when they try to correct our misconceptions.[36]

[36] http://www.npr.org/2012/03/21/149067359/how-race-shapes-national-health-debate.

"The tale of them" is a minefield to say the least, which is why my intuition that arises out of Ezra's and Nehemiah's marginalizing "tale of them" is (in the spirit of the aforementioned Sabbath ethic) that the privileged must learn to hear others' tellings of their own stories. Note the triple components of speaking, listening, and empathy inherent in the act of hearing one another.

> Everyone should get to tell their own story.

We've all heard the adage "to the victor goes the spoils" of war. One component of the spoils of war is the opportunity to tell what happened. The modern Western world saw itself as kinder, gentler, more evolved than those who came before, so we erected museums and filled libraries with volumes by which we catalogued and remembered the conquered. As a boy coming of age in Washington, DC, I would meander through the Smithsonian natural history museum and ask myself, "Who wrote the plaques in front of the exhibits?"

"All things, it is said, are duly recorded," wrote the mighty Ralph Ellison, "all things of importance, that is. But not quite, for actually it is only the known, the seen, the heard and only those events that the recorder regards as important that are put down, those lies his keepers keep their power by."[37]

[37] Ralph Ellison, *Invisible Man*, Special 30th anniversary ed. (New York: Random House, 1982, c1952)

The plaques in museums certainly weren't written by the people whose civilizations were decimated and put on exhibit. Was it anyone even remotely connected or empathetic to their story? How do we know what was said is true?

We don't. But what's important here is plurality, not certainty— breadth of perspective, not the indisputably right perspective. As novelist Chimamanda Adichie reminds us in her TED talk "The Danger of a Single Story," "Stories matter. *Many* stories matter."[38] It is far more important to offer better tellings of our stories than to lose ourselves in trying to correct every single mis-telling that's out there circulating. Like my Uncle Ralph once told me, "You don't grow grass by pulling weeds."

Historically, the stories given the greatest credence have been pretty one-sided. They were told from a particular perspective that reinforced a particular myth. That myth has proven to lack structural integrity. So, formerly colonized people don't have to try to be scientifically precise in telling their own stories— telling only those stories that can be proved beyond the Western standard of a reasonable doubt. That wasn't of primary concern before; it need not be of greatest concern now.

What's important is that we begin to tell our own stories. The public history work of Professor Tiya Miles, MacArthur Genius Grant winner for her research into Native American slave ownership, reminds me that as the formerly colonized we are just beginning to learn our stories for what they really are. With each telling, we will come to understand our own stories better.

Archbishop of South Africa Desmond Tutu speaks of the power of feeling truly heard for the first time. He witnessed it as he helped shepherd the Truth and Reconciliation process in post-apartheid South Africa:

> I was amazed, first of all, at how powerful an instrument it is being able to tell your story. I suppose psychiatrists understand that better than we. Just being able to tell your story. You could see in the number of people who for so long had been sort of just anonymous, faceless nonentities [the value of] just being given the opportunity for something to rehabilitate them.

> But it actually was a healing thing. We had a young man — a black young man who had been blinded by police action in his township, and he came to tell his story. When

[38] Adichie's presentation was given as a TED Talk in July 2009 at TEDGlobal conference Oxford, UK. It is a tremendous explication of a rationale for the type of work done herein and has garnered more than 3.5 million views and 100,000 Facebook likes since posted online. The complete thought from which the selected quote was taken reads as follows, "Stories matter. Many stories matter. Stories have been used to dispossess and to malign, but stories can also be used to empower and to humanize. Stories can break the dignity of a people, but stories can also repair that broken dignity."

he finished, one of the TRC panel asked him, "Hey, how do you feel?" And a broad smile broke over his face and (he was still blind but) he said, "You have given me back my eyes."[39]

The healing for the injured party didn't come with the simple admission from those who perpetrated the injury that the previous telling of the story was wrong. The healing came once the injured felt truly heard.

That's the rub, isn't it? It's hard for the privileged in any scenario to have their faults, shortcomings, omissions, malices, and continued privilege recounted to them repeatedly—which is what the stories of those who are injured tend to do (if only by implication). And as frustration with the process mounts, the response of the privileged is to want the injured to "just get over it." Ironically, that's all the injured want to do. But they can't if the privileged continue to accept the benefits of the system and structures that injured them.

Some may find the notion of refraining from telling others' stories absurd and unnecessary. To that I can only respond, yes, it is a gracious act of radical respect.

Ebony and Ivory

I have struggled up to this point not to address this concern in terms of black and white, because the intuition of hearing another's story has a power and beauty so much more pervasive than race relations. Colonizers and colonized both need practice truly hearing one another. However, the intuition of hearing the other directly addresses a problem that has an undeniably racial component.

It's hard to know how to speak to that racial component and, foremost, the prayer of a beloved community that makes room for all of us. I'll just come out with it, trusting you can hold both in tension.

In the colonized world, the authority to tell other people's stories was predominantly (though not exclusively[40]) the purview of persons of European descent. Maintaining that privilege of being the sole authoritative filter through which others' stories are told subconsciously perpetuates the notion that marginalized people were trivialized for a reason. Second, it connotes that the reason for marginalization was substantial enough that their retrospective interpretation of the experience lacks credibility.

[39] "[Unedited] Desmond Tutu with Krista Tippett," On Being with Krista Tippett, April 29, 2010, http://www.onbeing.org/program/desmond-tutus-god-surprises/85.

[40] Most of those who are not white grew up forced to learn the white portions of the Western story often before learning their own. So whether of European descent or not, the Western story is theirs as much as any other. Thus, when they speak of their Western inheritance, they can do so with an insider authenticity that isn't the same as when white people speak into people's of color experience. Still, we who have these sort of dual identities spoken of by W. E. B. DuBois learn the lessons of Western privilege well and sometimes perpetrate the offense on others, even white folks. The fact that all have fallen short, however, does not negate or lessen by degree how pervasively persons of European descent exercise their systemic privilege to tell other people's stories to others' detriment.

> "We must . . . take responsibility as a reader/interpreter/storyteller for the impact the stories we tell has on the lives of other women, men and children who hear them and try to live up to them."
> ~Renita Weems, womanist scholar

[41] Before including it here, I did raise my concern directly with those at *On Being*. I use this project I respect as an example of the irrelevance of intention in pursuit of beloved community, because I have faith that ultimately they can handle it well.

[42] Many of the quotations in this book are taken from *On Being* interviews.

[43] "[Unedited] S. James Gates with Krista Tippett," On Being with Krista Tippett, March 1, 2012, http://www.onbeing.org/program/uncovering-codes-reality/1457.

As an ultimate illustration I will critique a group of people for whom I have immense respect because I want to demonstrate that this is not about demonizing anyone nor is it about meaning well, it is about recognizing how deeply our thinking has been organized to privilege some tellings of a story over others for reasons that have nothing to do with the would-be objective measures to which we commonly appeal (authority, accuracy, simplicity, accessibility, respectability, etc.).[41]

As you might have deduced by now, I hold the people at *On Being* in the highest esteem.[42] For my money, it is one of the most interesting, well-produced and well-hosted talk shows on radio. Krista Tippett engages in intimate conversation with guests and asks the questions I hope I'd ask if I were ever as well informed. I love that the show often introduces me to people I may have never known otherwise but should. One such instance was Tippett's conversation with Sylvester James Gates.

Gates is a theoretical physicist specializing in supersymmetry, particle theory, and string theory. *On Being*, he described his scientific work:

> I'm one of the first people in the US to worry about this thing called supersymmetry, and I've been worried about it all of my professional life. We've never seen an experiment saying that, yes, I'm here in nature, but the mathematics has just been amazing. But there are problems that no one has solved yet in this mathematics.[43]

The fact that Gates can do math with ideas that exist only in theory basically means that, even when he's wrong, he's likely smarter than the smartest person you or I know. What I appreciated most about Tippett's interview with Gates is that had it not been for *On Being*'s intentionality about privileging often marginalized voices I may not have this example to share with my children of a contemporary science pioneer *who looks like them*.

Despite the accessibility of Gates's language, at the close of the unedited interview, listeners hear a pregnant pause to which Tippett responds to her production team that what they wanted felt too much like starting over. However, she does ask Gates if he has an elevator speech explanation of string theory. Gates's elevator speech didn't make it into the produced show, and wasn't especially missed. However, when the show aired, a link was advertised in the show and posted on the episode's webpage to a twenty-minute TED Talk on string theory given by Brian Greene that includes visuals.[44]

Greene, a respected scientist in his own right, has developed a name for himself as a public expositor of physics, appearing on-camera quite frequently. Greene offers a decent string theory primer, with visuals taken from a NOVA miniseries he hosted, *The Elegant Universe*, but what jumped out at me is that within the first forty seconds of his presentation, Greene contradicts Gates's ideas about the field of string theory that Gates himself helped establish.[45]

This is significant because what had been recorded wasn't some general program about physics. It was the story of S. James Gates, the leading savant in the area of supersymmetry (SUSY), the first person in America (possibly the world) ever to write a paper on SUSY (1976) nearly ten years before string theory (or Brian Greene) had any prestige, the first African-American to hold an endowed chair in physics at a major US research university, one of the discoverers and foremost expositor of Adinkra mathematics,[46] and so on.

Despite his obvious brilliance, as expressed via his accomplishments and his ability to expound on his field of study, someone felt that Gates's story could not stand on its own merits without Greene's clarification and, ultimately, contradiction. I had never seen *On Being* do that before.

Like the old folks used to say, "white folks' ice ain't no colder than black folks' ice." What Gates has to say isn't any more right, wrong or clear simply because Greene says it after him. It isn't like Greene restricts himself to magic one- and two-syllable words. Most of his analogies are quite similar to Gates's. In fact, his whole talk does little to further explain string theory; it's primarily about justifying his belief in extra dimensions. All Greene has in his talk that Gates doesn't are digitally animated graphics. But why would Gates? He was on the radio!

The folks at *On Being* meant not the slightest bit of harm; of this I am certain. In fact, the preponderance of the evidence suggests that their intention is to facilitate the intuition of a patiently cultivated *empathy* (the word for "learning to hear each other's story") that arises for me out of the Ezra and Nehemiah story.

[44] Gratefully it is no longer there.

[45] Gates doesn't believe there has to be extra dimensions beyond length, width, depth, and time for string theory to be true; Greene does.

[46] I'm not even going to try to explain! See http://www.onbeing.org/program/uncovering-codes-reality/feature/symbols-power-adinkras-and-nature-reality/1460.

[47] Like Beyonce's Lemonade demonstrates, you have to go through the intuition, anger, apathy, emptiness, accountability, and reformation before you can get to forgiveness, resurrection, hope and redemption.

[48] Albert Einstein's definition of insanity

However, like Honorée Jeffers points out, just because someone intends no harm doesn't mean they *do no harm*. In the beloved community we seek, there is undoubtedly a way to empathize with each other to the point that something so well meaning either becomes harmless or *goes undone*. But we have to be willing to put in the time. We have to be willing to wait—*as long as it takes*—for the previously silenced *to be and to feel* truly heard. Wishing we could just skip to the good part won't cut it.[47] It hasn't so far. And I believe another physicist once hypothesized that doing the same thing over and over expecting different results was the definition of something other than empathy.[48]

CHAPTER FOUR

Premonitions Regarding Identity

I know some great people. One of them is friend and musician Troy Bronsink. He is one of very few white men I've ever witnessed handle the trickiness of being "the only" in a situation by not reaching for his privilege[1] to assert himself and maintain his sense of identity. He didn't try to bully his way through the encounter behind the mask of his whiteness. He was kicking back with a number of black men and women sitting around a campfire sharing deeply and honestly about our experience as people of color at a wonderful yet very white Wild Goose Festival,[2] celebrating faith, justice, and the arts. I greatly appreciate Troy's genius in that moment, and pray that I walk in a similar grace when I find myself "the only" vis-à-vis those parts of my identity that carry with them historical privilege.

I often find myself being the only or one of a "representative" few "—in relationship to those parts of my identity that have been historically marginalized. Perhaps the reason why I don't resent it is because at a crucial moment in my development my uncle said to me, "Don't begrudge what makes you you." He went on to say something like, "If something about you allows you to move easily between different groups of people and enjoy things folks like yourself don't typically enjoy, that's okay. Use it." And that's what I've tried to do, particularly in situations when I could help someone understand the possible differences between theirs and another's story. But being in the space where that kind of intimacy could take place has meant being alone more often than I would have liked.

There are more than a couple white guys who I imagine could handle being in situations of radical minority, but of those I

[1] For example, the privilege of being the authoritative voice, the privilege of setting the terms of the conversation, the privilege of externally translating what was being discussed into something out of his own experience before being able to appreciate it, and so on.

[2] About 98 percent that first year.

> "If I didn't define myself for myself, I would be crunched into other people's fantasies for me and eaten alive."
> ~Audre Lorde, womanist scholar and activist

imagine who could, seldom have I seen them do it. Rarely do I see any white men in situations where they are the minority. Where there is one, there are usually several. In fact, there is usually a comparative majority (or is what I encounter less physical majority and more perceptual majority?), which we have to admit is an absolute statistical anomaly. White people account for roughly 25 percent of the world's population, and white women outnumber white men. What that means statistically is that no random sampling of the entire planet's population or of only white people would ever produce such a consistent encounter with a majority of white men as what I experience regularly. Absent the tendency for birds of a feather to flock together, statistically speaking, even in America, only two or three of every ten people I meet each day should be white men. But as mathematically indisputable as that is, that is not the case. Knowing this, I still find it hard to imagine white guys as running in packs. Seriously.

Like I can remember coming of age and realizing that girls flock together; they even go to the bathroom in groups. And, of course, we have the image of young black men roaming here and there in crews, and its raising some measure of concern—at least it did for the management of Abercrombie & Fitch at White Oak Mall in Virginia when I worked there as a teen. Every time two or more black young men would come in the store, they would page all associates to the front of the store.

> One day, a friendly fish swimming along greeted another saying, "Hey there, how's the water treating ya today?" To which the other fish suddenly panicked replied, "What do you mean? What the hell is water?"

But like I said, even the white men I know who function alone well don't do it often. More often than not, they find (or is it "seek"?) strength in numbers. In fact, one of the privileges to which I've been privy in moments of interracial intimacy is that, faced with likelihood of being in the numerical minority or any otherwise limited decision-making power, many of my white male friends find reason to opt out. The decision is seldom overtly racial, of course; but it happens nonetheless. So why doesn't it stand out? Is white maleness so much the norm in our frame of reference that we only take notice when the numbers of any other identity rise past a minimum?

Of course that is the case. A major part of the privilege of being in a social context designed by people like you is to privilege people like themselves. Your instinctual responses to almost anything is considered normative, whereas others' instinctual responses—even if identical to your own—can be seen as aberrant. Such a system traps some in a battle royale in search of a sense of self while freeing others from giving their identity a second thought, unless they choose to.

I, Too, Am Trayvon Martin

In his 1952 classic, *Invisible Man*, Ralph Ellison sought to give voice to this confusing vergence of societal realities. In the 1981 introduction, he was asked to contribute to a republication of the novel, Ellison explains:

> [Among the certain problems my protagonist raised] was the question of why most protagonists of Afro American fiction (not to mention the black characters in fiction written by whites) were without intellectual depth. Too often they were figures caught up in the most intense forms of social struggle, subject to the most extreme forms of human predicament but yet seldom able to articulate the issues which tortured them. . . . Therefore I would have to create a narrator who could think as well as act, and I saw a capacity for conscious self-assertion as basic to his blundering quest for freedom.

> My task was one of revealing the human universals hidden within the plight of one who was both black and American, and not only as a means of conveying my personal vision of possibility, but as a way of dealing with the sheer rhetorical challenge involved in communicating across our barriers of race and religion, class, color and region—barriers which consist of the many strategies of division that were designed, and still function, to prevent what would otherwise have been a more or less natural recognition of the reality of [our] fraternity. . . . Most of all, I would have to approach racial stereotypes as a given fact of the social process and proceed . . . to reveal the human complexity which stereotypes are intended to conceal.[3]

[3] Ralph Ellison, *Invisible Man*, Special 30th anniversary ed. (New York: Random House, 1982, c1952).

Ellison succeeds. He breathes deep humanity into the search for identity, without relentlessly vilifying those his protagonist struggles against. *Invisible Man* is the quintessentially human tale of finding one's self, despite the inability to escape forces hostile to one's very existence.

4 "People who believe themselves white"—as in believing themselves perpetually innocent in the enforcement of supremacist logic—as Ta-Nehesi Coates coined it in *Between the World and Me* (New York: Random House, 2015), 97.

> "The strongest lesson I can teach my son is the same lesson I teach my daughter: how to be who he wishes to be for himself . . . how to move to that voice from within himself, rather than to those raucous, persuasive, or threatening voices from outside, pressuring him to be what the world wants him to be."
> ~Audre Lorde, womanist scholar and activist

5 Jeremiah 5:21 and Mark 8:18.

6 Ibid.

The type of story Ellison wrote is not often told—a "dramatic study in comparative humanity"—at least it is not the story most often hyped. Baratunde Thurston's *How to Be Black* is one humorous attempt. David Lamotte's *White Flour* is one for the next generation. There are others. The comparison they draw is between a deep humanity that truly appreciates the myriad generative ways people can be in the world and a dominant culture (not an ascriptive group of people, but an antagonistic way of being[4]) that restricts us all to predetermined scripts of condescension and division.

Perhaps this type of story's lack of popularity is due to the fact that "comparative humanity" is not an easy story to tell. It requires unflinching honesty that most would rather avoid because it aims only to shed light and dispel shadows. Which means that some of what comes to light is decidedly unflattering. Ellison might have avoided it if he could. He had set out to write a very different novel, along very different lines that might have handled the issue of identity in a much more easygoing or more easily dismissible fashion than to frame it in the realm of invisibility. His handling, by implication, attributes to some "eyes that would not see"[5] (and by extension "ears that would not hear"[6]). The construct of invisibility generates immediate antagonism, which is not what a good author is supposed to instigate with his readers. But what could Ellison do? This was the story demanding to be told, because it was the story being despised, disregarded, overlooked—rendered invisible—by the dominant culture:

> While I [usually] structured my short stories out of familiar experiences and possessed concrete images of my characters and their backgrounds, now I was confronted by nothing more substantial than a taunting, disembodied voice. And while I was in the process of plotting a novel based on [World War II] then in progress, the conflict which that voice was imposing upon my attention was one that had been ongoing since the Civil War. . . . [The voice] seemed to tease me with allusions to that pseudoscientific sociological concept which held that most Afro-American difficulties sprang from our "high visibility"; a phrase as double-dealing and insidious as its more recent oxymoronic cousins, "benign neglect" and

"reverse discrimination," both of which translate "Keep those Negroes running—but in the same place."[7]

"Keep those Negroes running." Who are "those Negroes"? Are they a peculiar people or a proxy for any targeted for marginalization? What is their complicity, if any, in their ongoing marathon? Who is forcing them to run? What if the routinely marginalized realized that they could not outrun the dominant culture's misperceptions? What if they stopped, turned to face their accusers, and stood their ground?

Asking those questions. Moving sporadically, even simultaneously, toward and away from the issue of identity, trying to focus, reminds me of a similarly complex and layered story— the story of Esther, Jewish queen of Persia. In some respects, Esther's story is premonition of or down payment on[8] the Third Isaiah promise to give a name and a voice to aliens and orphans, women and eunuchs. All four are chronicled in Esther's narrative as exercising extraordinary visibility at a time when the dominant culture was insisting they have none. Esther's story stands in sharp relief to other biblical narratives of its time. The one shame is that this story of identity and self-discovery had to come at the expense of Israel's cultural independence, as opposed to being the gift Israel cultivated within her own borders "for the healing of the nations"[9] around her. Thank goodness the Hebrew storytellers did not resent that shame but saw this story as a gift and preserved it. Consider Esther's story as seen through the eyes of the often invisible.

The Helpers

The following is a brief series of diary entries, retrieved and compiled from the ruins of the royal courts of the Medes and Persians, telling the story of their second great queen. The list of chroniclers includes:

Criscos, former attendant to Queen Vashti; friend of the seven eunuchs that attend to King Ahasuerus; sympathizer with a plot against Ahasuerus.

Minimus, handmaiden to Esther, one of the seven maids appointed her by Hegai.

Mordicai, Esther's cousin who raised her; recognized as a Jew, but is fourth-generation exile; wants Esther to pass for Medeo-Persian.

[7] Ellison, *Invisible Man.*

[8] Scholars aren't sure of the timeline.

[9] The book of Revelation in the Bible includes this pretty prominent metaphor of people of faith finally united with God and becoming like a tree planted by a river of life whose leaves are for the healing of the nations (chapter 22:2).

Haman, high official of the Medeo-Persian royal court.

Esther, Jewish queen of the Medeo-Persian empire.

8th day of Anāmaka, the 10th month of the royal Persian calendar, in the 7th year of Ahasuerus

Criscos: That heifer—what's her name? Esther?—couldn't hold a candle to Queen Vashti (she will always be my queen), but she must have put it on ol' Ahasuerus last night! The king's eunuch said homeboy stumbled out his royal chambers panting, "Tell Hegai we've found our new queen! He can send the others home!"

I still can't believe Ahasuerus just replaced Vashti like that! It's been four whole years since he banished her! I thought for sure he would miss her after a while and beg her to come home. Just because she didn't want to be ogled by all the drunk, bougie friends he'd invited to come celebrate his third year as king. That was a sleazy move to put her in that position. Obey the king's summons and be objectified; disobey and incur his wrath. Secure your man's favor or abdicate your own dignity. What kind of choice was that?

Then for Ahasuerus to be goaded into banishing her by the bullshit his government officials were selling. They had him convinced that if he didn't make her suffer some serious consequences, Vashti's defiance would undermine the ability of "every man to be master in his own home." As the Jews say, "What a putz!" If a man has to flex his muscles to prove he's strong, he isn't as strong as he thinks he is.

Well, if that's the life his new little queen wants, she gets what she deserves! At some point he'll roast her on the altar of his ego too.

8th day of Tebeth, the 10th month of the Jewish sacred calendar, in the 7th year of Ahasuerus:

Esther: Queen? Oh, my! Really? Why am I so blessed and highly favored? And to think I didn't believe Father Mordecai, when he suggested that I could be the next queen. I almost refused to go when he told me he had gotten me in under the Persian name Esther instead of my Hebrew name, Hadassah. I still don't know how I feel about that. I know he means well. Even though he's really my cousin, I love him like my father because he's raised me from a toddler. If he has done me any offense, it is only that of loving me like a daughter and thinking of me as the ever naive little girl he raised.

Father couldn't have delivered me into better hands in the royal citadel of Susa. I don't know why Hegai treated me so well, providing me with such wonderful accommodations and seven handmaidens, including my precious Mini. At the end of our year of finishing school, which included in-depth instruction in the Kama Sutra, the one thing I was sure of was that I didn't know the half about being a queen, let alone a lover. I had believed Auntie when she told me, "No amount of practice can prepare you for marriage, yet no practice will guarantee you remain unprepared."

I was grateful several other girls had been chosen before me. I thought they might save me from ever having to face Ahasuerus. They weren't even allowed to come back to the maidens' chambers to tell us what their experience was like. Once with him, they joined the king's harem and one of the eunuchs came for their things.

Then the day came that the king called for me. As the hour approached, I became more and more anxious. All the girls who had gone before me were the most sophisticated and self-confident among those of us chosen. What would I be able to do to gain the king's favor that they could not?

Finally, about four hours before the evening meal, Hegai came to me and asked if there was anything I wanted in preparation.

"Only what you would suggest," I responded out of unguarded anxiety.

Hegai undoubtedly saw my angst. He sat me down and looked in my eyes with genuine concern. "My dear, by and large, men, even kings, are creatures of the hunt. Never underestimate a man's desire *to catch* his chosen prey—but they also like to chase. So don't surrender so quickly. The Kama Sutra speaks of husbands and wives waiting four days before sharing themselves with each other, to give love time to blossom. Ahasuerus may not wait four days; then again, maybe he will. It just depends on how good you are at making him think you are worth the wait.

"Most girls think their honey is so sweet it will blow the king's mind. But let's be real. As beautiful as your particular blossom may be, there is nothing you can do with it that he hasn't seen many times over in the same day (at the same time even). Any one of his concubines would count it the fulfilment of all their joys to delight him, if only for one night. But a queen must be the king's delight and so much more. To win his devotion, you must give him eyes to see the many other things that make you special.

"Most girls try to do too much and then get shuffled off to the harem. Others fall short in that they only use one, maybe two of the tools available to them. Remember what your teacher told you: 'Anticipation can be as sweet as acquisition.' So maybe on the first evening you leave him with a simple, yet passionate kiss and invitation to see you again. On the next day, maybe you should take a long stroll down to the river, eat and then bathe together. The next time you see one another, perhaps you massage and explore his body; learn what touches he likes, and finish with one of the hand techniques you've learned. Then on the next time you are alone invite him to explore your body and learn what touches you like. In this way you will teach him to think of you as one who matters.

"At this point, he won't be able to keep from having you, so enjoy yourself. After he's lain there empty for a moment. Put your head on his shoulder. Stroke his arms and chest. Talk to him gently. Invite him to share his heart. Listen. Wait until after he confides in you something few know about him. Then do something to alter the mood ever so slightly. Have the musicians to play softly from the next terrace. Call for fresh fruit, honeycomb, tea and a basin of hot water and a cloth. Begin to feed him as he continues to talk. Then, as he lulls into introspection . . ."

I came this close to ignoring Hegai's advice, even after asking for it. What would a eunuch know about pleasing a man? Oh, but that mutual velvet tongue business made our eyes roll back in our heads!

15th day of Tebeth, the 10th month of the sacred calendar, in the 7th year of Ahasuerus:

Minimus: I can only dream of a wedding day as fair. Oh, to be like Esther, beautiful Queen Esther who shone like polished sard in the sun: she was absolutely radiant.

I'm sure Queen Vashti's reign began with similar pomp and ceremony. I'm sure she made similar vows and had similar hopes. She and the king may have been truly in love at one time, and I'm sorry he lost sight of the demands real love never makes. But somewhere along the way Vashti also had forgotten some things. As mother says, "Being a queen is about more than what you say no to: it's ultimately about that to which you say yes."

Had both Vashti and the king remembered, today may never have happened.

21st day of Shebat, the 11th month of the sacred calendar, in the 7th year of Ahasuerus:

Mordecai: I have to get news of this plot against Ahasuerus to my Hadassah. The king may have his faults, but for my daughter's sake I must do what I can to forestall his demise. Bigthan and Teresh are soldiers of valor and high regard. If they lead this coup d'état, the ministerium, military, and the masses will undoubted ally themselves in a way that they may not for others. If the coup were successful, what would become of my Hadassah? She likely would be slaughtered in an attempt to snuff out all remembrance of the king. Despite any legitimacy of their grievances, I will not allow this.

Once she makes known this attempt on his life, if Ahasuerus has not truly loved his Esther before, he shall love her hereafter.

22nd day of Shebat, the 11th month of the sacred calendar, in the 7th year of Ahasuerus

Esther: If this had come at any other time, it would be much more difficult to manage. How will I explain how this news was brought to me? Everyone knows Mordecai is Jewish. I'll concoct a story about meeting Father upon my arrival at the citadel. I'll say, "Mordecai the Jew helped me when I was in distress and told me that I reminded him of his deceased wife."

One of the amazing things about being an occupied people is that it is easy to be overlooked. That is not a good thing, but every once in a long while it plays in one's favor. I have been to these very gates with my father as a child more times than I can count. If anyone at the palace had ever stopped to take any notice of us, it would not be so easy to keep my identity a secret. That's likely the reason why Mordecai was able to remain in earshot of Bigthan and Teresh as they plotted. Attendants are seldom given a second thought. It's a wonder they don't do more of the plotting themselves. Politics almost always puts the occupied just out of reach of the opportunity to affect real change—except when in service to the powers that be. Imagine how easy it would be for the occupied to physically rise up and overthrow their occupiers if they were so inclined. Alas, because political occupation includes occupation of the mind, few (occupied or occupier) see opportunities to live beyond their geographic and societal limitations. I surely didn't.

Now that I am beginning to, I have to keep practicing it—this impulse to be fully self-determining, fully human. The question is how.

5th day of Bāgayādiš, the 7th month of the royal calendar, in the 11th year of Ahasuerus:

Haman: My time has come. Teresh and Bigthan's assassination plot was the best thing that could have happened for me. Slowly, shrewdly Ahasuerus started distancing himself from the most prominent nobles in preference for younger, newer ones whose ambition could be easily converted into loyalty. My resulting ascendancy has been like the intoxicating fragrance of apothecary oils, awakening the ecstasy found in my mounting royal influence. Except for the one fly in the ointment—this Mordecai the Jew!

How dare he openly deny me the obeisance the king has decreed? Greater men bow in deference and homage to my office. This type of rebellious spirit will ruin our nation. We must preserve law and order. If everyone were allowed to be dismissive of the laws with which they disagree, society itself would descend into chaos and insurrection.

Inasmuch as he has publicly embarrassed me, I should have my guards grab him before all the people at the king's gate tomorrow, then take a sword and cut off his head with one decisive blow.

But that would be beneath my office to be so concerned about such an insignificant person. Plus, it might turn Mordecai the Jew into a martyr for his people and stir up repeated rebellions. But what if I could exterminate both him and his ilk from the empire? How?

I know. At the first of the year, the king will convene his chief officers and cast lots to assign a day pleasing to the gods to establish their legislative priorities. When lots are cast for me, I will introduce legislation against the Jewish seditious element within our midst. The day on which the lot lands would be the day all true Persians must rise up and execute all Jews throughout the kingdom. I'll even offer to finance the endeavor myself in the greater interest of the kingdom. Ahasuerus won't be able to resist that.

Then all people of the earth will know what happens to those who defy the authority of Persia!

13th day of Ādukanaiša, the 1st month of the royal calendar, in the 12th year of Ahasuerus:

Criscos: I know he's some kind of friend of the Heifer (Vashti will always be my queen), but that Mordecai is a cock-eyed fool. He was at the citadel gates today wailing at the top of his lungs, dressed in burlap sackcloth and smeared with the black soot of ashes. What did he think that was going to do? If he wants to do something about the decree Haman just signed, he better get the hell out of Susa as soon as he can and put a lot of distance between himself and Haman.

Speaking of Haman, that's one audacious bastard, going after an entire group of people just to settle a dispute with one! That's some shit, thinking to eradicate a people because they won't succumb to your crooked-ass way of being in the world. I bet he and the other chief officers sat around the table this morning wishing they had castrated all adolescent male Jews, like they did so many of us.

Do they think the people of Persia will slaughter their neighbors without provocation? What kind of people live in that kind of antagonism with all others around them and expect it not to come back on them? That is why I would have supported Bigthan and Teresh, fellow eunuchs from birth, if they hadn't been betrayed. Ahasuerus and his cabinet need to learn that chickens come home to roost!

13th day of Nisan, the 1st month of the Jewish sacred calendar, in the 12th year of Ahasuerus

Minimus: Esther is a Jew! I knew there was something kindred about her. It now makes sense why she would say, "There is not much difference between you and me," and would let me have Sabbath with my family and encourage me to speak our language and to honor our holy days. Now the exchange between her and Mordecai registers as more than dangerous impertinence on his part.

Esther sent Hathach out to Mordecai, who told him all that had happened and the exact sum of money that Haman had promised to pay[10] into the king's treasuries for the murder of the Jews. Mordecai gave Hathach a copy of the written decree issued in Susa to show Esther, along with his insistence that she go to the king to beg his mercy for our people. When Hathach told the queen what Mordecai had said, she sent him back saying, "All the king's servants and the people of the king's provinces know that if anyone goes to the king without being called, there is but one law—all alike are to be put to death. Only if the king holds out the golden sceptre to someone, may that person live. I myself have not been called in to the king for at least a month."

14th day of Nisan, the 1st month of the sacred calendar, in the 12th year of Ahasuerus

Esther: "Everything costs something—good or bad," Auntie used to say. Now I see the true cost of father's ploy: extortion. At first it was imperative no one know I am a Jew; now I am a traitor to my people if I don't come out in brash solidarity. When do I get to choose an identity for myself? Not that I want to see any harm come to my people, but identity politics is treacherous.

To hear Father tell it, we are all pawns in some cosmic Mancala game. Ironically, the way God is trying to move me always seems identical to what Father wants. Any other time Father would be cautioning me to be measured in my response. Now that his own life is threatened, it seems easier for him to demand I loose my arrow immediately, despite my lack of aim.

Mordecai: How can she not see her duty? It is as plain and as present as the noonday sun. This is time for aggressive action no matter the cost!

[10] $3 billion!

Choosing one's own identity is a fundamental exercise of one's humanity; conversely it is an act of indignity to impose a particular identity on another.

Did I make some mistake in my raising of her? Would she dissociate herself from her people in their hour of need? Can she not see the difference between expediency (for which I had her conceal her heritage) and abandonment?

She dare not think that she will escape the fate of her kinsmen just because she lives in the king's palace. If she keeps silent now, relief and deliverance will rise for the Jews from another quarter, but she and her father's family will surely perish.

Who knows? Perhaps she has come to royal dignity for just such a time as this. I will tell her when the sun is up!

16th day of Ādukanaiša, the 1st month of the royal Persian calendar, in the 12th year of Ahasuerus

Criscos: I didn't think the girl had it in her. I thought for sure she would just give in when Mordecai started prognosticating about her obligation to her ethnic heritage, but she refused to be pushed around. She took her time to think things over (she even asked me what I thought). When she was ready, she had Hathach instruct Mordecai, "Gather all the Jews to be found in Susa, and hold a fast on my behalf; neither eat nor drink for three days, night or day. I and my maids will also fast. After that I will go to the king, though it is against the law; and if I perish, I perish." With that Mordecai finally stopped all his damned signifying and took his ass home to do as he'd been told.

19th day of Nisan, the 1st month of the sacred calendar, in the 12th year of Ahasuerus:

Esther: I will go before Ahasuerus unbidden, because it is within my power to do so. And whomever I'm supposed to be, I choose to exercise the power to do good on behalf of more than myself as a part of it.

What was it my teacher used to say about anticipation and men being "creatures of the hunt"? I have to link my appeal to Ahasuerus's desire to be desired. Let him see how much I've missed him and remind him of how much he's missed me.

I'll invite him and Haman to dinner this evening and lull Haman into a false sense of security while I subtly remind Ahasuerus of how loyal and valuable I and several other Jews are who have taken governmental posts since the failed coup. I'll just bring up their names in conversation, failing to mention anything about their ethnicity. Ahasuerus is a smart man—when he's not drunk— he'll connect the dots. If my charms serve me well, I may have him disposed toward rescinding his decree before I even bring it up.

20th day of Nisan, the 1st month of the sacred calendar, in the 12th year of Ahasuerus

Minimus: You should have seen Haman this evening, hanging on Esther's every word, laughing at all her jokes, applauding her every notion. In that moment if someone had told him who she was, he likely would have responded transfixed, without the slightest clue of the deep irony, absurdity, obscenity in his words, "She's different. She's one of us."

It reminds me of the excessive attention a random few occupied persons get when someone who is not really pro-occupation but who haply or happily benefits from it realizes that occupied people can be extremely talented. All of a sudden, it's like, "Wow! I never thought someone like you could do something like that. That's amazing!" when, whether done exceptionally well or not, it's really just human.

Criscos told me he heard that, after Haman's banquet with the queen, he called his friends and his wife, Zeresh, together and drunkenly recounted to them his abundance and how the king had advanced him above the other officials and the ministers of the kingdom. Criscos told me he said, "Even Queen Esther let no one but myself come with the king to the banquet that she prepared. Tomorrow also she invites me, together with the king. Yet all this does me no good so long as I see the Jew Mordecai sitting at the king's gate." Then supposedly Zeresh and all his friends said to him, "In the morning have your servants erect a gallows 29 meters high, and go ask the king to have Mordecai hanged on it. Then go with the king to the banquet in good spirits." Haman was so excited he commissioned the gallows immediately. His servants have been working through the night, without sleep. I have to tell Esther when she awakes.

21st day of Ādukanaiša, the 1st month of the royal calendar, in the 12th year of Ahasuerus

Haman: I can't believe the king would humiliate me so! How was I to know the king was thinking of Mordecai when he asked me what he should do for one whom he wanted to honor! I had hoped he was thinking of me. What king goes back into the annals to be reminded of a debt of gratitude he owes? I never would have suggested a horse and robes, had I known. My wife and friends say this is a bad omen for me.

22th day of Nisan, the 1st month of the sacred calendar, in the 12th year of Ahasuerus

Esther: So the king and Haman came to visit again. We were drinking wine after our meal, and Ahasuerus asked for the third time in two days, "What is your petition, Queen Esther? It shall be granted you. Even to the half of my kingdom, it shall be fulfilled."

Finally I answered, "If I have won your favor, O king, and if it pleases the king, let my life be given me—that is my petition—and the lives of my people. For we have been sold, I and my people, to be destroyed. If we had been sold merely as slaves, men and women, I would hold my peace, but no enemy can compensate for this damage to the king." (You just have to love all that courtly talk.)

Then Ahasuerus said to me, "Who is he, and where is he, who has presumed to do this?"

To which I responded "A foe and enemy: this wicked Haman!"

Haman was terrified! Ahasuerus jumped up livid and stormed into the palace garden, but Haman stayed to beg his life from me. He knew the king had determined to destroy him. "My queen, I did not know," he kept saying.

"Even if these were not my people," I scolded, "you would have been wrong."

When Ahasuerus returned to the banquet hall, Haman had thrown himself on the couch where I was reclining. Ahasuerus then demanded, "Will he even assault the queen in my presence, in my own house?"

Then Criscos Harbona, one of the royal eunuchs, who I would have sworn despised me, said, "Look out the window, O King. There are the very gallows that Haman has prepared for Mordecai, whose word saved the king." And Ahasuerus said, "Hang him instead." So they hanged Haman on the gallows he had prepared for Father.

As we lay in bed tonight (oh, yes, I thanked him royally), Ahasuerus asked me why I had kept my true identity from him for so long. I could only answer with a question, "Would you have embraced me as all I am had you known?"

The More Things Change

My telling of Esther's story is substantially midrash intertwined with the biblical narrative. Yet I imagine a context in which what is recorded in ancient text would make sense because context shapes meaning. In that sense, my efforts are not very different than those of an actor as described by Sidney Poitier in his spiritual autobiography, *The Measure of a Man*.

As I experience the Esther diaries I can't help but be overcome by certain premonitions about identity. For one, it is a fundamental exercise of one's humanity to choose one's own identity. Perhaps the converse is also true. It is an act of indignity to impose on another a particular identity. It renders them invisible, a metaphor which in itself almost explains why identity is such a difficult issue to talk about in terms other than protest. What terms don't relentlessly pit us-versus-them and not alienate us-and-them from everyone else? When talking about identity, we're talking degrees of light and dark that not everyone can or wants to see.

> People should be accepted for acting out of whatever generative identities they choose, at whatever times they choose, and to whatever degrees they choose to embody them.

If self-identity is a basic human dignity, then it stands to reason that people should be accepted for acting out of whatever generative identities they choose, at whatever times they choose, and to whatever degrees they choose to embody them. At no time should we hold someone hostage to our perceptions of who they are.

Now that may seem remarkably self-evident to some, but take a moment and think of how often we hold people to our perceptions and what problems it causes. Whether it's parents expecting their children to pursue a particular career path and marry a person of a particular pedigree or employers expecting employees to avoid certain political affiliations, as negotiators of late-modern society we do it all the time. Think of the pain caused to persons coerced into living a lie because the choice for them is dignity or opportunity, not both. Consider the sheer time wasted in critiquing someone else's representation of self because that person somehow doesn't measure up to our suffocating expectations. And recognize how particularly thorny it all gets when we do this to whole people groups.

I don't know what it is, but the Western world seems to oscillate between not wanting to acknowledge identity (in terms of difference in experience) to wanting to reduce many different identities into one objectified identity group: the Muslims, the Evangelicals, the Gays, the Blacks. The trick is that the power to identify in both instances resides outside the subject. It's "Beauty and the Beast"—you are what you are perceived to be—and it has functioned to devastating ends.

Take, for example, the Melungeons of Appalachia whom DNA testing has conclusively linked to African heritage. On one hand, this is a great thing, to begin to know from whence one comes. On the other hand, consider the myths that would have caused a group of people to collectively deny that part of themselves so many years ago. Generations of Melungeons have lived under the misapprehension that the color of their skin had no relationship to anything African. They asserted they were of Portuguese descent or Native American descent, but definitely not African, with their narrow features and straight hair. Not that Portuguese and Native American lineages are less worthy; but what dreadfulness, what brutality, made a lie preferable? "You can be dark as long as you're anything other than African." Being of African ancestry makes one no less Melungeon. As the late Irish poet and philosopher John O'Donohue noted, "Your identity is not equivalent to your biography."[11] But oh, to heal the wounds that wantonly sever one's identity from one's biography—from one's biology—for some dominant cultural delusion.

[11] John O'Donahue, interview by Krista Tippett, *On Being with Krista Tippett*, Krista Tippett Public Productions, Minneapolis, Minnesota. Available at www.onbeing.org.

I find particular evidence of an achievable something better in the life of Sidney Poitier. In the chapter of his spiritual autobiography entitled "Life in Black and White" (an allusion to race and to the times during which he graced the big screen), he eloquently unpacks this business of finding dignity in integrative self-identification. In one section he recalls a lesson learned from an unlikely teacher in the late 1940s:

> My teachers came in a wide variety of forms and in a great variety of locales. Louise, for example, lived in Brooklyn, and the trip from the American Negro Theater

on 127th Street in Harlem to her doorstep was a long ride. I offered to see her home one night after a late rehearsal at the theater, and I would wind up making that trip time after time.

Saintly, volatile, edgy, raucous, bitchy, introspective, sensuous, a talented and daring taker of risks—that was Louise. In acting class she was a riveting, hypnotic presence. As a nineteen-year-old black girl, she was often mistaken for Arabic, or Asian, or Native American. She was, in fact a mixed-race person of African-American and white descent, but she claimed only her African-American heritage. . . .

We got locked in a conversation once, I remember, about who she was and who I was, as individuals, in America. "How we see ourselves, how we see each other," she said, "should be determined by us and not by people who generally don't like us; people who pass laws certifying us as less than human. Too many of us see each other as 'they' see us. . . . Time for that shit to stop. We're going to have to decide for ourselves what we are and what we're not. Create our own image of ourselves. And nurture it and feed it till it can stand on its own."[12]

[12] Sidney Poitier, *The Measure of a Man: A Spiritual Autobiography* (New York: HarperCollins, 2009).

Like the story of the Persian Queen Esther, Poitier offers some intuitions of the good accomplished when one gets to finally own one's identity on one's own terms and speak out of whatever parts one regards as pertinent in the moment.

One such good is that you come to appreciate you for you. You begin to see your choices in life, your agency. Life isn't just happening to you; you become response-able. You can at that point learn to be true to yourself and false to no one. Another such good is that you are free to appreciate others for who they are. They have value beyond your agreement with them. If you're fortunate, you begin to recognize that their shadow side is no more or less problematic and a potential blind spot than your own. Who knows, you may look up one day and say in effect like Tony Curtis's character in *The Defiant Ones* (costarring Sidney Poitier), "There's much about me that is you, and there's much about you that is me, and I'm comfortable with that."[13]

[13] *The Defiant Ones*, 1958, directed by Stanley Kramer.

Let me acknowledge that a lot of our lack of appreciation for others' choosing their identities lies in what we see as core moral discrepancy between our own identity and theirs. It's not that we fundamentally dislike the other person. We just think they're going to hell or are otherwise morally compromised in a way that makes us fearful. It's hard to accept, let alone appreciate that which one finds fundamentally flawed—essentially at odds with everything one believes to be right. Is there room for Hamans in our more appreciative world? I think so, as long as his continued participation in society isn't allowed to threaten that of others. But wouldn't that be a useful rule of thumb applied to us all?[14]

But how might we live with all this plurality of identity, moving toward appreciation of one another? The thoughts of Kwame Anthony Appiah—whose parents, interestingly enough, were the inspiration for Sidney Poitier's *Guess Who's Coming to Dinner?*—may offer some assistance:

> The key change is when you come from thinking of an issue as being about homosexuals and Muslims [or politics and race] and come to think of it as being about, you know, Uncle John and Aunt Mary and Cousin Ahmed. It's not Muslims; it's these particular people now and it sort of gives it a kind of concreteness. Sometimes people think that...the only way to deal with these big differences between religions or around moral questions is to kind of face up to the difference directly. But I think often, as it were, sidling up to it is better. And sidling up to it can be done by not facing Islam, but facing Leyla and Ahmed and Mohammed with whom you don't talk about religion most of the time. You talk about soccer or you talk about...rock music or whatever it is that you have in common as an interest.

> And the thing that binds me across, say, religious boundaries to people on other sides of religious boundaries isn't one thing, right? What binds me to Islam is my Sunni friends and my Shiite friends, my Ismaili friends, my cousins who happen to be Muslim, and strangers whom I've come to know and like who are Muslim. And what I have in common with these very diverse group of Muslims that I know is different in each case. So that breaks up the sense of them as a kind of monolithic "them."[15]

[14] Too bad Mordecai doesn't learn this later on in Esther's story.

[15] "[Unedited] Kwame Anthony Appiah with Krista Tippett," On Being with Krista Tippett, August 4, 2011, http://www.onbeing. org/program/sidling-difference/175.

[16] Krista Tippett's description of Appiah's work, ibid.

[17] Okay, maybe not all five aspects of this last one, but you get my point.

[18] See http://www.npr.org/2012/07/06/156373488/-will-same-sex-romance-sink-r-bs-ocean.

Appiah's work pushes at the idea that we are all composites of many different identities (parents, children, friends, lovers, etc., all-in-one), and he describes "human flourishing writ large as having difference at its core and not as something that is overcome, but something that is always there and part of vitality."[16]

So I have made a new acquaintance who is an African-American female preacher, born and raised in the Deep South, exploring the possibility of living a raceless life. I also have a Philly-grown, guitar-playing, former praise-and-worship leading Korean friend who knows far more about hip-hop than most black folks I grew up with. I even know a white dreadlocked religious conservative, and straight female athletes who are bald and atheist too.[17] Hopefully what I learn to appreciate in them carries over in my dealings with others who, too, claim some aspect of my friends' identities.

Bringing my thoughts full circle, let me lastly suggest that part of the dignity of self-identification should be that it does not call into question one's common humanity: the right to speak to that identity without disqualification and the right to speak beyond that identity without relegation. NPR special correspondent Michel Martin points out that this is not always the case with, let's say, black journalists when they report on issues regarding race.[18] Their blackness is seen as immediate bias. It can also happen to women speaking to gender issues and LGBTQIA persons addressing sexuality and gender expression.

In a round-table conversation about the news of the day, the observation was made that Anderson Cooper is better positioned than most in that he can still trade on his white maleness in a way others cannot, though he has now come out publicly. That may be true, but it doesn't have to be the last word. So comedian Chris Rock tweets, "Happy white peoples Independence Day the slaves weren't free but I'm sure they enjoyed fireworks [sic]." His blackness shouldn't disqualify him or relegate him from speaking to an ongoing dissonance in how different identities experience America differently.

Several years ago I heard mainline church historian and thinker Diana Butler Bass talk about the grace required in accepting, even appreciating, each other's varying identities:

> When I'm in rooms of clergy and theologians . . . and we
> start talking about post-conservatism and post-liberalism

. . . I always remind them that those "posts-" come out of a very distinctive historical experience. And those historical experiences are always going to remain part of our identity. They don't just go away because... [we] say we want to be friends. We're going to be standing in our conversations having coffee[, and] I've got Schleiermacher standing with me all the time, not John Stott. If we think about that conversation happening not just here and now but in that larger communion of saints... [it's important to recognize] we are opening up conversational space for people who once killed each other. That is very gentle [work], and you can't just say, "That never happened!"

We're going to be doing this convergence work, but holding onto the things that we love and the things that make us who we are.... It is a potential, terrible misstep for people who have been schooled in liberal Protestantism to let go of their identity for the sake of one happy, big family.... We need to be who we really are . . . but it doesn't mean we can't form something new together.

Change the context by switching the religious ideological references to any other identities, and the gist of her argument remains credible. Despite the fact I bring Nathaniel Hawthorne, Nat Turner, Geronimo, Harriet Tubman, Frederick Douglass, W. E. B. DuBois, Paul Robeson, Langston Hughes, Zora Neale Hurston, James Baldwin, Sonya Sanchez, and many others to the park bench with me, and you might bring George Washington, John Brown, William Lloyd Garrison, Robert E. Lee, Abraham Lincoln, and/or Ralph Waldo Emerson, and another might bring Benito Juárez, Frida Kahlo, Paulo Freire, Delores Huerta, Isabel Allende, Esmeralda Santiago and/or Julia Alvarez, we can form something new together.

My intuition is that, in order for it to be better for more than just a privileged set, the intuitions of beloved community we've found in these first faith stories will have to be a part of it. And like abandoning the impulse to draw circles and learning to listen to others' stories of themselves, appreciating others' self-identification doesn't cost much except our own pretenses about what is certain in the world and what isn't.

CHAPTER FIVE

A Sense of Ownership

I realize the courageousness of a world exhibiting the intuitions of beloved community arising out of the previous three stories may seem a bit lofty. I tend to think that much of why we end up with much the same from generation to generation is because we aim too low. Nonetheless, it may be useful if we search for a few less ambitious intuitions to help us scaffold up to the big ones.

On December 23, 2011, while heading back home to Atlanta from Christmas shopping with my children in suburban Douglasville, we were delayed in our endeavor by Cobb County's finest.

For those who don't know, Cobb County, Georgia, is like mini-Texas—willingness to secede and all—a world unto itself. (The county seat, Marietta, is pronounced by locals as "May-retta). Starting in 2017, Cobb will be home to the Atlanta Braves,[1] whose owners flatly refuse to end the sacrilegious commercial use of the tomahawk (a Native American sacred icon) in their logo and team cheer. Among the reasons offered by team executives for moving out of Atlanta into Cobb is that Cobb is not only "near the geographic center of our fan base" (whatever that means), but "access around the stadium . . . [will be] greatly enhanced"[2] by the county's lack of public transportation and highest concentration of daily rush hour congestion in the metro area. But I digress.

Needing to stop for gas on my way home, I had taken a quick detour through the neighborhood into which my oldest two, my daughters, were born. The following is my best recollection of the unwelcomed interaction that ensued:

"Good evening," came with a most cheerful tone and grin. The officer was rather tall and stayed just behind my door so I had to crane my neck to see him. Because of his height, he had to stoop

[1] Don't miss the irony.

[2] Tim Tucker, "Braves Plan to Build a New Stadium in Cobb," *Atlanta Journal-Constitution*. November 11, 2013. http://www.ajc.com/news/sports/baseball/braves-plan-to-build-new-stadium-in-cobb/nbpNQ/.

to see me. In a manner that caught me completely off guard, the officer had brought his hands together in his lap and did that half sit-squat that one might associate with a very genteel host from a 1950s movie showing delight or surprise while talking to someone about waist high.[3] "The reason I pulled you over this evening is that one of your taillights isn't working."

"I didn't know."

"Well, good. If you had said, 'It's been that way for about a week,' we would have had to have a very different conversation (mutual chuckle). Well, consider this a verbal warning. Now if you don't mind letting me check your driver's license, I'll let you be on your way."

While he looked at my license, we made that very purposeful small talk in which police engage, but the quirky cheerfulness in his voice made it quite disarming, plus he kept his flashlight out of my eyes. "Where are you headed this evening?"

"We were headed back home from Douglasville. I needed to stop for gas. So I decided to take my kids past our old house."

"Do they all have their seat belts on?"

"Yes."

He and I both inspected the backseat.

"Well, let me run back to the car to check and make sure you're not a felon wanted in fourteen states (chuckle), and I'll be right back."

Upon his return a different voice greets me, because it's a different officer. Officer "Jolly" is still there, now in full view, about ten feet away from my car door, beaming his goodwill to all, in that most wonderful time of the year. Replacing him closest to me is a noticeably less jovial sort who feels the need to reiterate a few things. "Okay, Mr. Bray, do you know why we stopped you?"

"One of my taillights is out." I glance up at him, but he's standing so that the searchlight from his cruiser is in my eyes. I note the cop scowl on his face. Now that's what I had initially expected. I look back down at my license in his hand. "I'll stop on the way home to pick up a new bulb."

"And do you know the way back to the interstate?"

"Sure." I glance over at Officer Jolly. He is still grinning and nodding. "I used to own a house right down the hill where we lived when my two—"

"Good." And with that he hands me my license and walks away.

In all honesty, he may have bid me goodnight, I truly don't remember. It is most likely that his partner did, but by this time I was wrapped up in my own thoughts. With what has been a 50/50 chance of officers approaching me with guns drawn, I was just thanking God that I had avoided the worse for my children's sake.

I'm not the quickest guy. I don't pick up on insinuation right away. Even if I had noted something askew in the moment, I likely would not have addressed it with my kids in the car. But as I pull off, the implication of the final question posed by Officer "Grim" is slowly dawning on me. What did he mean, "Do you know the way back to the interstate?"

As I pump my gas, I'm wracking my brain for the context in which "Do you know the way back to the interstate?" would have no subtext to it, and shy of having expressed some confusion about where I was I can't figure one. Couldn't he just have been trying to be helpful? Sure. Even if you discount the fact that the interstate was less than a half-mile in the direction I had been traveling and would be visible within fifty yards. Remove all possible negative intent, and one is still left with the suggestion, "You don't belong here."

> Equity begins when we recognize our power to not accept anything but.

How is such thinking even plausible in twenty-first–century America?

"Of Course We're Nothing Like That"

There is a lot of innovation happening within faith traditions today. Within Christianity, much of that creative energy in the first decade of the new century coalesced into referring to itself as the Emerging Church. Diversity was a big part of Emerging Church conversations in the United States. However, in a manner typical of the various modern institutions we emerging-types were so fond of critiquing, after all the talking, diversification simply did not occur within emerging circles to any great degree. Gatherings frequented by emerging-types were just as monochromatic as gatherings in most mainstream Christian events. With full knowledge of the sincerity with which so many desired diversity and inclusion, I know it was disheartening.

Over time I've heard friends resign themselves to an idea that might be articulated something like this: inclusion's charge to us is to invite and welcome others into our home. And whereas that may be an important lesson in hospitality, the virtue of inclusion appears to want to teach us a somewhat more challenging lesson.

I would argue that we persist in the problems that we have with race relations in the United States today, not because of the color of anyone's skin; but rather, because of power and our love of it. Our stubborn refusal to relinquish it. One reason I was drawn to the Emergent Village conversation (one particular manifestation of Emergence Christianity) was that when I attended my first Emergent cohort gathering at a bar in Decatur, Georgia, the convener, a man of strong Dutch lineage who since has become a wonderful friend, said to us newbies, "Many of you are here to have someone tell you what the Emergent conversation is about." It was all very *Matrixy*.[4] "What I want you to know," Troy Bronsink continued, "is that the Emergent conversation is about whatever you choose to contribute to it this evening. It is what you shape it into."

That statement blew my mind. In all my years of growing up in an interracial church, attending a predominantly white elementary school and learning to be comfortable transgressing racial boundaries, I had never heard a white man, friend or stranger, give power away. That may strike some as an extremely racial thing to say, and it is. It is one of those stark differences in experience that most people of color have from most whites in a still very intellectually, emotionally, and culturally colonized world. If you're having a difficult time accepting this statement as self-evident, ask yourself why (within the West) the language of "minority" still brings to mind a person of color, despite the fact we supposedly live in a global society that happens to be three-fourths people of color.[5] Or try to give a coherent explanation for why in the twenty-first century it remains uncommon to find even proportional demographic representation between leadership and membership of any social institution? Yet it is still quite common to find white men in almost perpetual leadership of groups in which they are minimally represented. The Christian church is the primary case in point.

[4] Think Neo and Trinity speaking for the first time in the nightclub.

[5] Not to overlook the deeper truth late civil rights activist and scholar Vincent Harding points out, "In community the concept of 'minority' simply doesn't work. You don't have a 'minority' in a family."

Because this act of giving power away was so dramatically unfamiliar to me, I was immediately seduced. Whatever they were smoking, I wanted some—even though I've never smoked. Emergent eventually became my tribe. Emergent-types were the people I felt most at home with spiritually. At one point, I even became a co-convener of Emergent Village's Village Council, which at the time fulfilled the organizational necessities of a board and a program committee.

It was in the wake of that experience that I recognized how difficult it is to see privilege from the inside. I was able to articulate that only after stepping down from that post. Whereas our conversation had been great at helping folks who wanted to live more generatively "get off the grid" as it were, our conversing had done very little to address the big issues of power, equity, inclusion, and so on that had driven folks to want to get off the grid in the first place. Because we had not in our time together built more sustainable systems, the social dynamics of our middle-aged capitulation, as we now form churches of our own, pay bills, and raise kids, look very similar to those we railed against in the fervor of young adulthood.

The Ties that Bind

In light of how difficult it is to see beyond one's privilege, I am reminded of two stories with seemingly opposing outcomes. The first is the story of Ruth, which actually begins with her mother-in-law, Naomi, who, along with her husband and two sons, were Hebrews from the land of Israel. A famine had come to Israel and had driven Naomi's family into the land of Moab in search of food. Israel and Moab had a long antagonistic, maybe even codependent history. They fought back and forth for centuries, with intermittent times of peace. One might say this is typical of family, and they would be right, for both the Israelites and Moabites traced their lineage back to a common ancestor, Terah, Abraham's father. Lot, Abraham's nephew was the father of Moab, by his eldest daughter—a whole other story.

Naomi's sons grew up in Moab and married natives Ruth and Orpah. Life for the three women proceeded, as one might expect, until one after the other, their husbands died. With no more blood family left and the famine having long since subsided in her own country, Naomi decided she wanted to return home.

> "The ache for home lives in all of us, the safe place where we can go as we are and not be questioned."
> ~Maya Angelou, author

There's something about home that has meaning. There's something about home that makes intuitive sense. I don't have to figure it out. I don't have to overthink my words. For example, if I happen to get angry—there are some things worth being angry about, you know—it's okay. They don't feel compelled to read into it.

Naomi wanted to go home. This, of course, saddened Orpah and Ruth. They loved her. She was a link to their deceased husbands. They had no desire to lose that.

The way the story is handed down to us. Naomi decides she didn't need anything but the clothes on her back. She was going home. The Hebrews had all sorts of wonderful legal/cultural provision for how they dealt with the widow, the poor, even the foreigner, so even if no one recognized her, she would be okay. All she would have to do was make it back.

The younger women decided to travel with Naomi to the border of their territory. It was likely several days of walking, but they didn't mind.

At the Moab border it was time to say good-bye. Orpah and Naomi kissed and embraced. Their tears mingled on their cheeks. They didn't want to let each other go. Orpah understood how Naomi felt, because she couldn't imagine dying in a place that wasn't her own. She loved Naomi. She had loved Naomi's son. But she could not imagine leaving the love she felt for and from her own people. She wondered how Naomi had done it for so long. But since the famine was no longer a threat in Israel, why stay in Moab?

Naomi and Ruth's moment of embrace was no less torturous. Would they ever see each other again? Would they ever even hear news of how the other was doing? As they held onto each other for dear life, afraid of what would happen should they let go, Ruth had an existential crisis. To the applause of generations who've thought it a mere trifle to abandon one's own upbringing and sense of self, Ruth utters some of the most famous words in Hebrew scripture, "Where you go, I will go. Where you lodge, I will lodge. Your people will be my people, and your God, my God?" Woo-hoo!

Ol' sorry Orpah, though—the ingrate, the ignoble savage—how dare she have concerns that did not make Naomi the center of her world? Doesn't it just make you feel all warm and fuzzy on the inside to think that Ruth would give up everything for Naomi? Kinda makes you think the Israelites (the ones with whom we generally identify) must have had it going on! Or that the Moabites (the other) must have been pretty lame to lose one of their best to us. She must have been one of their best, because she marries into money and prestige and becomes the great-grandmother of the great King David, thus part of the lineage of Jesus himself. How could one be more fortunate?

And on the strength of that we say to the "others" among us, "Why don't you feel welcome? I've invited you. I've smiled at you. I've patted you on the back. I've even sung some of your songs in ways that you don't recognize! Why don't you feel at home?"

Ruth and Naomi's story turned out really beautiful and all. Ruth "married up" as we say. But I have to hold that story in juxtaposition to a story like Hagar's. She was slave to Sarah, matriarch of the Jewish people. Number one, Hagar didn't ask to be a slave. (Who does that?) She was trafficked from Egypt. Women weren't valued, so the idea of just trading a woman— "Hey, take her"—was just part and parcel of how things went in antiquity. As a son, brother, husband, father, friend—one defined by  relationship to the women in my life—it makes me shiver. Hagar was given away to Abraham as a so-called sign of respect from Pharaoh. The irony of an Egyptian giving a slave to a Hebrew would be comical if not so tragic.

Abraham leaves Egypt on the way to the land Yahweh (a name for God) has promised to show him. They are in the desert, and they have this prophecy that Abraham would be the father of many nations. The prophecy, as handed down to us, doesn't really pertain to Sarah. So we can't say whether her faith is weak at this point or if she's just trying to calculate the shortest distance between two points. But she says to Abraham, "Listen, I can't give you a child. My womb is obviously dead, and even if it weren't true before, I'm eighty-plus years old. What are the chances that I'll get pregnant? Why don't I extend the wrong perpetrated on this child, Hagar, when she was given to us to be taken to a land she knew not of? I'll give her to you so you can conceive your first child before you're too old to get up for the occasion."

It's amazing how easily one can make decisions that involve the fate of others without even a thought about, let alone a conversation with, the person who picks up the bill for our actions. I love the way Caroline Kennedy, a writer who once participated in a *Stories that COMPOST* writing workshop I facilitated, describes Hagar's situation. "It wasn't quite rape, but it wasn't quite not rape either."

I think Caroline is too kind. It was rape, but for which there was no acknowledgment of a crime, because (think *The Jeffersons*) Hagar was "movin' on up (movin' on up) to the east side (movin' on up) to a dee-luxe" compartment just off Sarah and Abraham's master tent. And the fact that Sarah is involved makes the scenario a little less morally repugnant, doesn't it? If wrong was done, it can only be incidental (right?).

So Abraham takes Hagar and forcibly impregnates her. (Again, these are not Hagar's choices.) She is among a people who have welcomed her. She has gone from being a slave to being a concubine, "wifey" if you will. This is a step-up. Shouldn't she be overjoyed? And now she's pregnant! Who knew whether she wanted to be pregnant? Did it even matter to Abraham and Sarah (or anybody else in their community) whether or not she wanted to be pregnant? But she's pregnant with Abraham's child and now she's dealing with drama from Sarah, the sanctimonious woman who gave her to him!

> "When someone shows you who they are, believe them the first time."
> ~Maya Angelou, author

Sarah's all like, "She looked at me funny."

And Hagar's like, "I'm done. I don't need this." And since she's risen from the status of slave, her captors—our heroes—aren't watching her as much, so she breaks.

Of course, the way we have historically told the story is that the angel of the Lord came and told her to go back. Maybe. Not everything in the Bible with which God's name is associated is an act of God. If you take exception to this statement, go to the idea of the conquest of Canaan, the story of Joshua and Judges. The way we traditionally tell that story is that Yahweh told the Israelites (Abraham's "legitimate" children) to wipe out all the people of Canaan (some of whom were Abraham's "illegitimate" children or cousins a few times removed). What's nonsensical about attributing the genocide command to Yahweh is that, before we get to the books of Joshua and Judges, the book of Deuteronomy issues all those rules about how to treat the alien and the stranger and members of "the mixed multitude" that came out of Egypt. In Deuteronomy we learn how to take a slave and bring that person into the family, and then to give that person the same legal rights and the right to inheritance and a voice (vote) among the people. If Yahweh wanted Israel to wipe out everyone who wasn't like them, then Yahweh's Deuteronomic description of inclusive society doesn't make sense.

So it seems sometimes we claim God in things that God is not. In fact, I'm sure of it.

Anyway, Hagar comes back and gets about the business of raising her son in a hostile environment. If mistress Sarah has issue with Hagar, you can be certain that others loyal to Sarah see her as the wounded party, particularly when they see Abraham interacting with the boy as . . . well, a son. Consequently, the boy's mother benefits from the deference afforded the boy, which reinforces Sarah's sense of injury.

The boy is strong. The boy grows. His name is Ishmael. He grows. He's a hunter. He loves his mother and his dad, and they love him.

Meanwhile, Sarah gets pregnant and has a son whom she names Isaac. Ishmael loves his little brother, Isaac. One day he's out doing what big brothers do, giving the little brother a hard time. But somehow, when we give each other a hard time, challenge each other across lines of difference, there's all this subtext.

I remember years ago I went to have an introductory meeting with the principal of the school where I was later to do my student teaching. This also happened to be the school attended by many of the students I previously had worked with at the local Boys & Girls Club. It wasn't quite time for me to start my student teaching. I was actually there because the principal was going to allow me to volunteer in the school as a representative of the faith-based youth development organization Young Life.

Early in our conversation the principal, a white woman, began bragging about the school's racial diversity. It was the only public school in the Huntsville, Alabama area, that was about 50 percent white, 30 percent black and 20 percent Asian and other. She was so proud of how well everybody got along. I was impressed. So I asked what I thought was a reasonable participatory question, "How many people of color do you have as teachers?"

We had what was (to me) a nice conversation. I was an education major, and she was schooling me as to the realities of working in the field. It was very pleasant. Then I left.

I had a ten-minute drive back to the Young Life offices. By time I made it back to YL, my boss (a white man) who attended the same church as the principal who just interviewed me needed to speak to me. He said with the kindest smile, "Yeah, I just had a phone call from the principal over at the school. She was wondering what kind of hidden agenda you may have for working in the school, like you were planning to cause some type of racial dissension or something." (The layers of subtext were so thick you would have needed a chainsaw to cut them.)

> "History, despite its wrenching pain, cannot be unlived, but if faced with courage, need not be lived again."
> ~Maya Angelou, author

My boss had no desire to offend me. I had no desire to offend the principal. I'm sure she had no desire to offend my boss when she called. But someone, something had undoubtedly been offended. Of course, the only explanation I could offer was that the principal had started the conversation; I was just participating. Because of the love my boss and I shared, I think he got it. But it is the nature of interracial uncertainty that all the subtext between us is not really knowable. (Did he get it—that this is the bullshit that will forever haunt the halls of systems of inequitable power that are never dismantled? Or did he just excuse it, chalking it up to my youth, inexperience, or reasonably good intentions?)

So there was all this subtext Sarah was seeing, or thought she was seeing, between Ishmael and Isaac, and she told Abraham that Ishmael (and his mama) had to go. Abraham responded as any father should, "No, I can't do that." Yet the way the story is handed down to us, Yahweh says, "Abraham, you have to get rid of them."

I've thought long and hard for a rationale that makes this just. What I have come to is that it was better that the child not grow up under the tyranny of Sarah. Having seen the results of integration into a social system in which power remained secure in the hands of others, this makes sense to me.

Whatever the rationale, Abraham came to some conclusions about the situation, and banished Hagar and Ishmael to the desert. That's the secret fear of everyone who is not like you, and why they are wise not to fully trust your welcoming them into your home. As long as you retain power, you have the ability to throw them out when you're not happy anymore. That's why only a few people take the risk.

God Bless the Child That's Got Her Own

If we are going to tell a more beautiful story, my intuition is that those who have it are going to have to give up their "power-over"—the insider's power over the outsider, the old's power over the young, the rich's power over the poor, men's power over women, white people's power over people of color. The privileged, whoever they may be, have to put themselves in a situation where it's not *their* home anymore. It's going to have to involve incredibly intentional gestures that violate some of our most deeply held myths. For example, every interest represented in the room having equal (not proportional) decision-making power. Or even better, those who have traditionally had power willingly choosing to go along for the ride and letting someone else drive.

> Power-over dynamics must become power-with, a new type of shared ownership.

Pottery artist Simon Levin, an ethnic Jew married to an Episcopalian priest raising interfaith children in the Midwest, once put it to me this way, "You have to move beyond extending invitations to extending ownership." He was speaking of a festival I was helping to curate, but it seems to be salient advice for any venture in the global society in which we now live. To invite diversity without shared ownership simply broadens one's sphere of potential, perhaps inevitable, injustice.

Think about that for a moment. Try to imagine an instance when it has not been true. Call a friend who did not have ownership stake in the instance of which you are thinking and ask them how they experienced it.

I would argue that this inevitable injustice is what happened with the American civil rights movement and is the reason why so many of our best efforts at enfranchisement since remain dogged by dismay and defeat decades later. Concerning the 1954 *Brown v. Board of Education of Topeka*, the US Supreme Court ruled "separate educational facilities are inherently unequal." Separate is unequal, so we insist on integration. What the sound bite of our historical memory does not consistently convey, however, is that separate is inherently unequal, specifically within systems where power over one persists in the hands of another.

Remember the question I asked in the first section of this chapter? The only context in which the distrust of cross-cultural subtext is neutralized appears to be that in which all parties recognize themselves as being adequately resourced before engaging.

Though the circumstances of the landmark ruling were brilliantly portrayed by Sidney Poitier in the made-for-television movie *Separate, But Equal*, not even he got at this core truth therein. Ironically, though, Poitier is still the one who convinced me of this truth through his spiritual autobiography. He attributes his ability to engage anyone he encountered in Jim Crow America as an equal to his security in knowing he had his own elsewhere—his own language, his own culture, his own property, his own stories, etc.

In the stories of faith that have been handed down to us, amid all the other things going on, many of which are certainly unworthy of emulation, we can find the beauty of what happens when people see themselves "caught in an inescapable network of mutuality, tied in a single garment of destiny,"[6] as in Ruth's story. However, we would be more than disingenuous to ignore the more than occasional stories like Hagar's in which characters with whom we often identify have in no way been worthy of such trust. Nor can we remain ignorant to the many necessary and brave course corrections that had to be made in the time between Hagar and Ruth—several hundred years.[7] It wasn't just a matter of Ruth getting past everything that had happened to her, nor was it about Naomi living in perpetual guilt or apology.

One of many corrective measures taken over the years that separate Hagar and Ruth were those very commands of inclusion, equity, wealth distribution, and power distribution recorded in Deuteronomy. They were part and parcel of that which was, over time, to set Israel apart as the shining "city on a hill" among other nations. These are very similar to the opportunities (some

[6] Martin Luther King Jr., "Letter From Birmingham City Jail," 1963.

[7] Don't get it twisted: that says nothing prescriptive about how long change should take.

embraced, most squandered) we've had since the time of MLK's death to make strides in what it means to be a multi-racial, multi-ethnic, multi-religious democratic nation. Vincent Harding names the elephant in the room related to the issue of ownership that hinders true equity, diversity and inclusion:

> One of the deeper transformations that's going on now is that for the white community of America, there is this uncertainty growing about its own role, its own control, its own capacity to name the realities, that it has moved into a realm of uncertainty that it did not allow itself to face before. Up to now uncertainty was the experience of the weak, the poor, the people of color, that was our realm. But now for all kinds of political and economic reasons, for all kinds of psychological reasons, that uncertainty and unknowingness is permeating what was the 'dominant' (so-called) society.

> I think that's the place that we are in and that's even more the reason why we've got to figure out what was [Martin] King talking about when he was seeing the possibility of a beloved community and recognize that maybe for some of us that cannot come until some of us realize that *we must give up what we thought was only ours* in order for all of us to find new possibilities in the building of a beloved nation.[8]

The idea of giving up is one that most of us can't even fathom. Even hypothetically, how could we go about giving the land taken in our terroristic invasion of the US territory back to the First Nations? I can't begin to wrap my brain around it. But the intuitions of justice arising out of these highly regarded ancient stories of Hagar and Ruth seem to demand something be given, which is why I press into this sense of shared ownership. In extending ownership, "power-over," our failed mythology, is traded for "power-with," a much more just, feasible, and coherent way of being in a post-colonial world.[9] But it is not something that should be expected to come easily to us. "When it comes to creating a multiracial, multiethnic, multireligious, democratic society, we are still a developing nation. We've only been really thinking about this for about half a century, and there's still so much that we don't know."[10] So we'll have to give each other lots of grace.

[8] "[Unedited] Vincent Harding with Krista Tippett," On Being with Krista Tippett, February 4, 2011, http://www.onbeing.org/program/civility-history-and-hope/79.

[9] Word constructs so artfully advocated by Robert Jenson in his book *All My Bones Shake* (Brooklyn: Soft Skulls Press, 2009).

[10] "[Unedited] Vincent Harding with Krista Tippett," On Being with Krista Tippett, February 4, 2011, http://www.onbeing.org/program/civility-history-and-hope/79.

11 William H. McNeill, "The Care and Repair of Public Myth Foreign Affairs 61, no. 1 (1982): 1.

Though perhaps more radical a pronouncement than widely entertained by any but the aggrieved, the intuition of extending ownership is a line of reasoning one might expect from a book like this. However, I remained chastened by the hope of Martin Luther King Jr. echoed in the redemptive longing historian William McNeill expressed in his article "The Care and Repair of Public Myth" published in the *Foreign Affairs* journal in 1982. McNeill yearns that we find a way to fit our new "sensibilities into a wider perspective in which weak and strong, or oppressor and oppressed would all find a place."[11]

Thus, I would be remiss not to acknowledge that at least one other intuition arises out of these stories for me. Whether or not the privileged initiate the move from power-over to power-with, the un- and underprivileged can still recognize their "power-to." Another word for power-to is *agency*. Agency is the power to effect change simply by living into it. As Gandhi advocated, one can be the change s/he wants to see in the world.

Agency isn't granted: it's taken. Of necessity, otherwise it is only permission and can be restricted. It starts as an internal disposition. It then grows into a refusal to be treated (or to respond) in any way except the manner desired. When I say refusal, I'm not talking about an attitude, as in an emotional state. I'm talking about a personal integrity, an incorruptibility, an unflappable commitment, much like I've encountered in every Buddhist I've ever met.

Harding points out that it was this very sense of agency that drove the song leaders of the marches from Selma to Montgomery in March 1965 to declare for themselves, "This little light of mine, I'm gonna let it shine!" Instead of meeting a less than gracious Gov. George Wallace with commensurate indignity—a man whose lips King iconically described as "dripping with the words of interposition and nullification"—these heroes of transformational change saw their opportunity to claim their own dignity despite what others might do.[12]

12 "[Unedited] Vincent Harding with Krista Tippett," On Being with Krista Tippett, February 4, 2011, http://www.onbeing.org/program/civility-history-and-hope/79.

In like manner, we, too, have agency to embrace a sense of ownership that transforms every encounter into one that affirms everyone's blessed and unique humanity and right to belong. What better *means* by which to declare our intention "to be a human being, to be respected as a human being, to be given the rights of a human being in this society [whatever the society, organization, religion, tradition or nation may be], on this earth, in this day?"[13]

13 "The context of the often misinterpreted El-Hajj Malik El-Shabazz (Malcolm X) "by any means necessary" quote. See https://www.youtube.com/watch?v=mnJWQb0PjVM."

CHAPTER SIX

Notions of Privilege

I refuse to be a minority. Such language serves no purpose, as Vincent Harding notes, in a human community that ever hopes to be democratic, let alone beloved. Though at first rooted in the realization of its factual fallacy, of late my resolve against the minority label has little to do with numbers. At this point my resoluteness is a denial of the very premise of majority-minority and similar constructs. Like Pulitzer Prize-winning journalist William Raspberry, one of the very first black journalists to have real impact and a genuine following in the so-called mainstream media, I'm saying (with identity points particular to me, of course):

> If you ask me, "Am I an African-American first or a male first, or a Mississippian first?" I'm me first. I'm all of these things. I'm black, I'm short, I'm old, I'm Southern. I'm reasonably sensitive. I'm a husband and a father and a pretty loyal friend. And I'm all these things mixed up, and I have given up trying to separate them out into "Who am I the most?" I'm mostly me. And I feel pretty good about that.[1]

[1] Bill Raspberry in interview with Michel Martin for NPR http://www.npr.org /2012/07/18/156972589/ the-late-william-raspberry- a-role-model-and- more?sc=emaf.

I am a follower of Jesus, a person of color, a husband, a father, a friend, and so on all mixed up, with all the attendant challenges and benefits that come along with it. And I feel pretty good about that.

My resolve has served me well in that it has spared me from or deconstructed in me many of the psychological effects of being reared in and continuing to navigate a society designed to privilege folks other than myself. That does not mean I don't often hit walls for which I struggle to account. It means that I don't immediately look for race to explain those walls. And even at

"I am not tragically colored...."

[2] "I am not tragically colored." Zora Neale Hurston, *Dust Tracks on a Road* (originally published 1942 New York: J. B. Lippincott).

those times when race is the only explanation left, I don't see who I am as something to be overcome simply because it does not entitle me to the privilege from which I find myself momentarily excluded. In many ways I am myself privileged not to have my sense of self and possibility dictated by external definitions and realities, for if Zora Neale Hurston is right,[2] life favors those capable of writing their own story.

Privilege does not limit itself to issues of race. It can also manifest, for example, vis-á-vis experiences—experiences that open doors. For reasons I cannot account, I've gotten to do things and meet people about which others dream. In most instances I was not alone, which means there are plenty of others as fortunate as I. So perhaps my experiences are not as unique as they are diverse, having the tendency to cross boundaries of experience that are often not transgressed. This is privilege, affording me opportunities that many others will never have.

Privilege seems to revolve around many axes—race, gender, age, socioeconomics, nationality, ethnicity, culture, religion, experiences, interests, and so on—almost simultaneously, like a gyroscope, and can turn one's mind topsy-turvy trying to isolate which axis of identity accounts for the most significant privilege at any given moment. An equally confounding question is how to reverse the privilege already set in rotation without toppling social systems. Perhaps a better question in this instance would be how we can draw more and more people into the privilege we've found, recognizing that any advantage worth having is worth sharing with everyone.

Worth a Thousand Words

Sometimes what is privileged is a particular way of thinking:

Barry Deutsch

Dana Simpson

The thing about each of the above graphics is that each of them implies a winner and a loser, an insider and outsider, a person privileged by the dominant way of thinking and being in the world and one who is not. It doesn't take great mental acumen to recognize who typically advocates the privileged point of view. It's quite often my own so-called Christians. So I couldn't help but wonder how those who have staked such a claim on the person of Jesus could so often be found on the side of a privilege Jesus regularly spoke against and be absolutely comfortable with it.

Then one day a potential explanation came to me. I was making a quick run to my school on a Saturday morning, absentmindedly listening to a local gospel radio station, when a beautiful song came on about how great and mighty God is. I find it difficult nowadays to stomach most popular praise and worship music, but this song immediately took me back to those days when I found the sentiment being expressed deeply meaningful. As I hummed along, I kept wanting the song to go somewhere beyond the repetition of "how mighty is our God," but it never did. The lyrics never said, "Because our God stands above all things, we can forgive . . . or hope . . . or love without limit!" There was no "since God is greater than any setback I might encounter, I can finally, as the Bible says, 'Do justly, love mercy, walk humbly' in the world.[3]"

[3] Micah 6:8 ESV.

In the disappointment of the moment, I was struck by the prevalence of the God the Conquering Warrior motif in so much of the music of my upbringing. "Onward, Christian Soldiers!" "[God] has loosed the fateful lightning of his terrible swift sword." "The Lord is a warrior; the Lord is mighty in battle." "We are soldiers in the army (of the Lord); we have to fight although we have to die."[4] As the titles and verses washed across my mind, I couldn't help but wonder: What type of religion does such iconography shape? Why would people with that God on their side—wanting them to triumph over all others in every circumstance—ever stop to consider the possibility of being wrong about anything, particularly their understanding of God and who God expects them to be?

[4] "Onward Christian Soldiers, "The Battle Hymn of the Republic," "Warrior," "We are Soldiers in the Army"—all songs of my youth.

In a thought-provoking installment of the now discontinued comic strip called *Russell's Teapot,* atheist Chaz Bowman points out the lack of empirical evidence that "the secularization of America is directly responsible for the majority of our societal problems," a way of thinking often privileged by people of faith. Bowman utilizes as a backdrop the photo of a group of what appear to be kindergarteners sitting on the floor in their classroom, with a teacher and the main character of the strip, Russell, drawn in. In true fundamentalist fashion, the teacher, who bears a passing resemblance to Dana Carvey's church lady, suggests to the class that things would be so much better had we not as a nation turned our back on God. Russell, who can't help but think critically, asks about Norway. In answer to the befuddlement of his teacher and classmates, Russell proceeds to run down a list of chart-topping statistics related to quality of life in Norway, which he notes has arguably the world's most godless society. Very politely, the teacher thanks Russell for the information he has shared with the class. Then, before he can take his seat, she quips, "I hope they speak Norwegian in HELL!"

Even in the face of incontrovertible refutation, we get to maintain whatever constructs privilege us, right?

Louder Than Words

All this talk of privilege reminds me of one called Zacchaeus, who had a privilege-altering, random encounter with Jesus one day. Jesus was passing through the ancient trade city of Jericho, headed back toward Jerusalem and, apparently knowingly, to his death. Zacchaeus strikes me as a man who'd want to tell his own story, so I'll let him.

"I know how my people feel about me. (Shay, more food and drink for my guests.) I am a publican, a tax collector. In fact, I am the superintendent of customs! With all the balsam produced and exported from Jericho for perfume and medicinal purposes throughout Gilead, Palestine, and beyond, there's no way I wouldn't be rich. The absentee nobles who own the large corkwood estates that produce the most myrrh and balm understand it as the cost of doing business. Tenant farmers despise me, as if this wasn't the way business has been done all their lives. (Zeporah, run to the neighbors and invite them over. Then have Oren take a wagon to the market and buy as many pillows as he can find for our guests.)

"I remember when I got the promotion. I thought, *Well at least I can now afford to distance myself from these peasants who begrudge my success.* But it didn't work. My wife and I have to interact with them one way or another every day. Their resentment is palpable. (Pass these bowls along so more people may partake, both in here and out on the veranda.) So when I started to overhear stories that you are one who doesn't discriminate against anyone—clean or unclean, learned or unlearned, Jew or Gentile—and are teaching others to do the same, I secretly hoped your generosity included rich and poor and wanted the chance to encounter you for myself.

"Everyone coming into the city this morning had word on their lips of what you did for that blind man. (Here, here, there's more room over here.) I was excited to learn you were coming this way. At my diminutive stature, there was no possible way I was going to be able to put eyes on you at street level. (Have you seen this crowd?) I thought to just wait on my rooftop, but I'm ashamed to say, there was a part of me that didn't want anyone to see I was taking interest. So I decided to climb that sycamore fig tree. Since figs are in season, I figured the leaves would obscure me enough in my green robe that no one would notice.

"You should have seen me trying to get up there—I'm not as nimble as I once was. (Anyone for more wine?) I eventually eased my way out on a branch. I had just gotten situated when I saw the crowd rounding the bend. (Haddaus, you must cook like this more often!) I figured it would pass beneath me, I could eavesdrop a bit and life would continue much as it had, for better or for worse. You can only imagine my surprise when you stopped right beneath me, looked up and called me by name! I hadn't noticed your glancing up along the way. I was so stunned I almost fell out of the tree. The idea that you would want to come to my home is beyond comprehension to me. (Shay, get Zaporah and Haddaus and you come sit down and eat with us. You can't do all the work; I'll help. You must have some of this!) The rumors are all true. But I don't know what to make of them.

"What does it mean to 'seek first the kingdom of God?' And what's this business about rich and poor, Jew and Gentile, clean and unclean being saved? All I know is that this is the first in a long time someone who wasn't beholden to me in some way or wanted something I have has visited in my home or broken bread with my wife and me. We don't have children, so at home all we regularly see are each other and Zaporah, Haddaus, and Shay, our servants (and I must confess, regrettably, I have not treated them well). But now (May I fill your glasses?), I no longer feel cut off. I no longer want to nurse my bruised ego by separating myself from others with my things. With just this brief interaction,

I'm no longer convinced everyone would do what I've done if they were in the same position.

"I want to find a better way of being in the world, Jesus. I will start by living up to my name. My parents named me 'pure,' yet I have been everything but that in heart. All my wealth, I have earned at the expense of others. Oh, I earned it—no doubt. I invested shrewdly in the wealth-generating opportunities around me. I put in long hours that brought in lots of money for my Roman employers. I did everything expected of me, and everything I did was fully legal, but that says nothing as to whether it was just. Roman law runs a different course than the ethics of this kingdom of God of which you speak, I know. So I want to chart a new course for myself. (Huh? I know, I know, we need more food. Go back to your pots, but at least set some aside for yourself. Thank you, Haddaus.)

"First thing I want to do is share my means with those who have none. I'm not just talking about giving money away. I want to help people find ways to provide for themselves. I will work to make all the businesses I've invested in employee-owned so that workers can share in the wealth the business creates.

"I know every businessman in the city. I know all they've done to get ahead and stay on top. I will use that knowledge to negotiate some, shall we say, 'tax cuts' for them for employing more workers and paying livable wages. I can even link tax collection to annual income after Temple taxation so that the

> "If this is going to be a Christian nation that doesn't help the poor, either we have to pretend that Jesus was just as selfish as we are, or we've got to acknowledge that He commanded us to love the poor and serve the needy without condition and then admit that we just don't want to do it."
> ~Stephen Colbert, satirist

nobles and merchants' attempts to recoup profit on the back end, in collusion with the Temple priests, won't undermine the tax relief I provide. (Shay, tell the people outside more is coming.) I know I can't stop all the corruption in Jericho that relegates some to abject poverty groveling in the shadow of obscene wealth, but I can stop being complicit in it.

"The second thing I need to do is make amends to those I've exploited for my own gain. I will let it be known that, if any lacks because of me, I will make restitution four times over. If that person has died, but their children are still without, all they have to do is let it be known, and I will extend to them their inheritance. From now on, in whatever ways I can (for with all this I likely will not be chief publican for very long, even if tax revenues don't drop much), the way of this 'love your neighbor' kingdom of which you speak will be my way as closely as I can imitate it. (Do you all want any more to eat?)"

Jesus smiled at Zacchaeus, the man who had been speaking. Then he turned to those who were traveling with him and sharing in the feast Zacchaeus was providing and said, "I told you only a day or two ago that it is easier for a camel to go through the eye of a needle than for a rich man to embrace the kingdom ethic. But despite the difficulty, with God all things are possible. You have witnessed today the transformation I said was required, which is why you can't ever write anyone off. Zacchaeus, too, is a child of Abraham: one who sees he has been blessed to be a blessing to others."

What Goes Around

Many reading this story may not be familiar with the context of the reference to Abraham that Jesus makes and what became of it. Over half of those who claim faith in the world trace that faith back to Abraham, an ancient Sumerian who relocated with his family from Ur (near the tip of the Persian Gulf) to Canaan (now Israel, Jordan, Lebanon, Syria and Palestine) in the pursuit of what he believed to be a promise from God that through him all the families of the earth would be blessed. Abraham was so faithful to that way of being in the world that despite the tribal aggression common to that time and that region, he moved a battalion of people that distance, by way of Egypt, without recorded incident. The Abrahamic ethic of "blessed to be a blessing," embraced and abandoned cyclically by his descendants, eventually gave rise to the best intuitions of what we now know as Judaism, Islam, and Christianity.

In terms of our attempts to tell stories that COMPOST, it seems fitting to let the story rest here, even though portions of the end of our telling are actually recorded as prelude to the Zacchaeus encounter in scripture. By emphasizing the continuity and connections, we certainly do confess more than we proscribe. We also acknowledge the deep others-interestedness threaded throughout scripture. By recognizing the inability for Zacchaeus to see everything clearly right away, we raise as many questions as we answer, particularly about our traditional assumptions regarding what it means to follow Jesus. By implication, we also put opposing interpretations of scripture in conflict with one another. And in doing each of these things, we treat the tradition as a bell still ringing, not a bell rung long ago. Those seem to me interpretive elements that our posterity can still wrestle with generations from now. They may not be able to or desirous of composting our interpretation of the story completely, but at least there's room enough in the telling for them to CO-PO-T their own ideas along with ours.

Because to this point in the Jesus story no one but Jesus has engaged in such explicitly radical generosity, it would be easy to dismiss Zacchaeus's reaction to Jesus as aberrant. However, we see it again as the immediate response to Jesus's ascension when his followers go to Jerusalem and live communally until the day of Pentecost. The ethic continues to persist as the number of those who begin to claim the way of Jesus grows exponentially in defiance of Nero, the then Caesar. Perhaps most dramatically, we see the same ethic demonstrated by Jesus's twelve closest male disciples who are now leaders of this new thing called "the church" that is emerging. In response to the "minority" Greeks' complaint that their widows were being neglected in the daily distribution of food in Jerusalem, the "majority" Jewish followers of Jesus voted for seven Greeks to oversee food distribution for everyone—thereby giving up the rare Jewish privilege to be in authority.

Some might argue that it was only through this having "all things in common"—provisions, property, power, privilege—that Christianity was able to subvert and survive Roman persecution. Remember this was the same Rome that had exerted her will from Europe, through the Mediterranean region of North Africa and on across to Asia. This was the same Rome that had squashed all attempts at rebellion and lined their roads with the dismembered bodies of publicly executed rebel leaders. This was the Rome that had successfully crucified Jesus. Had it not been for followers of Jesus extending themselves as the rule, not the exception, to an ever-widening circle of people, all of whom they could not have had prior dealings with, the way of Jesus may not have survived.

Then, about five hundred years in, things changed. Constantine came to power as emperor and "converted" to Christianity, seeing in it a way to unite a slowly fracturing Roman empire, and suddenly the once persecuted were on top. Constantine changed nothing about what Rome was, only whom Rome considered friend and foe. There was a new world order, and "the rest," as they say, "is history." Christendom thoroughly enjoyed its many days in the sun.

So here Christians are today. We sing, "Jesus paid it all" to create the possibility of "a new heaven and a new earth." When pressed, most of us will acknowledge Christianity has not done terribly well with the privilege of power and influence it has had for the past 1,500 years. We like to off-load some of our shame by clarifying that the worst offenders (it's a sliding scale) were, of course, not "real Christians." Still there is the matter of all the privilege Christians have accumulated for ourselves at the expense of others over the centuries. We find ourselves in a very awkward position, not metaphorically dissimilar to Zacchaeus caught out on a limb in a sycamore tree.

Knowing how the Zacchaeus story plays out, it is difficult not to rush to the inevitable question: Must present-day Christians, like Zacchaeus, give back all we accumulated under the former order to live into the new? If so, it would seem pretty straightforward that those privileged by current systems of inequity should dismantle the structures of inequity we've tried to preserve for fear of how vulnerable a new order might leave us. But there's a problem. There are so many myths we've been rehearsing over the years to absolve ourselves of any guilt we might have felt over the benefits we've derived from injustices perpetrated on our behalf. One of the major myths that stands in our way is the notion that *what's done is done: one can't change the past.*

And because there are so few examples other than those mentioned above of social orders or organizational dynamics not built upon oppressive inequities, because there are so few who have risked such a radical restructuring of thinking and practice as that advocated by Jesus and embodied by Zacchaeus, those of us who have reason to believe something better is possible in the here-and-now postpone it until some distant point in an idyllic future, when happiness and peace will subdue us against our wills and not be dependent upon our good-faith energies toward maintaining them.

> **Privilege is meant to be leveraged on behalf of those who have less privilege.**

C'mon! Is that all we're left with once we find the error of our ways? In light of Zacchaeus's story, I would dare say no. In light of Zacchaeus's story, I would dare suggest that privilege is not ours to enjoy but ours to exploit on behalf of others. And here is where it gets really tricky for Christians, for we love the stories and would love for everyone to sympathize with them even as we do, but we really don't want to be obligated to their costing us anything.

Ignoring the Obvious

I don't know what to say about that except, thankfully, it does not speak about all who claim Jesus. My guess is that there are plenty, from many different faith traditions and no faith tradition at all, who can immediately see the value in this intuition of privilege being ours to exploit on behalf of others. It seems almost self-evident, which is why it boggles my mind that in the twenty-first century a simple thing like gender equity can still be an issue of debate in the world! And if at this point in human evolution we can't be all for as basic a thing as gender equity, no wonder we can't come to terms with marriage equality, living wages, and religious pluralism.

Consider the fact that in 2016, American women still make less on the dollar than men, despite the Lilly Ledbetter Act of 2008. Over a lifetime at the median full-time earnings, that's approximately half a million dollars. What sense does that make? We have been depriving more than half the people in the country (women and children) what they need in order to do more than survive. We weren't supposed to applaud as James Brown crooned, "It's a man's world;" we were supposed to see the dirt on our faces in the mirror of his melody and go wash it off! But that would be too much like right.

> "When you're accustomed to privilege, equality feels like oppression."
> ~Brian Sims, member of the Pennsylvania House of Representatives

Heretofore, one could possibly accuse me of preaching to the choir about that of which they were already convinced or of trying to generalize my own personal experiences far too broadly, but here, in matters of privileges afforded some and not others, is where the rubber meets the road. What all need to understand is that obstinately maintained inequitable thinking is a problem long before it can be shown to be rampantly discriminatory, because by then the privileged have too much riding on current systems and it becomes too easy to maintain the status quo with myths like, "Oh well, we can't change the past without discombobulating the present."

So when politicians and other privileged persons get up and say, "There is not enough evidence to support such a claim or to justify the cost of such a drastic restructuring," they are so far beside the point as to be in another zip code. The fact that at least one human being is experiencing harmful repercussions from our chosen course should be all the evidence necessary to call our thinking into question. The question isn't: What's the minimum damage acceptable to get or maintain the privilege I want? All that does is create inequity and resentments that inevitably lead to war. For reasons that are self-evident and that appeal to humanity's noblest virtues, the better intuition is: What can we do to bring more and more into a privilege we all can share?

In September 2009, husband and wife journalists Sheryl WuDunn and Nicholas Kristof published a book on the issue of gender equity titled *Half the Sky: Turning Oppression into Opportunity for Women Worldwide*. The couple refer to "the struggle for gender equality in the developing world" as the "paramount moral challenge" of this yet young century. One after the other they set forth startling facts and figures as well as deeply compelling narratives of women fighting the good fight in the name of untold others around the world. And the true numbers are indeed untold, because if the authors are correct, calculations of male-to-female ratios reveal that at least sixty million girls and women are "missing" from global population figures. This gap, they say, is largely due to decades of gender-specific abuse, neglect, and infanticide or abortion, which the authors term "gendercide."

As appreciative as I am of WuDunn and Kristof's work, it makes absolutely no sense to me that in this day, one has to make multilayered, over-substantiated arguments for why women should be treated with the same dignity as men. Their basic argument is that educating girls and women is a dramatically cheap way to boost a country's economy. This to me seems like a no-brainer. But my question is: What if it doesn't? What if providing equal opportunity for education and employment to all women in the world doesn't produce one more lousy red cent for any man anywhere? Does that leave us willing to abide this foolishness one moment longer? Are you fuckin' kidding me?!

Sure we can point at sex trafficking/forced prostitution and gender-based honor killings or mass rape and astronomical maternal mortality in different places around the developing world and shake our heads. But back home in the so-called developed world we have commercial sexual exploitation of children (same thing, different name), legislators shaping public health policy based on notions like the female anatomy's ability to "self-abort" automatically in situations of "legitimate rape," and religious institutions, like the denomination of my childhood, still embroiled in debate over whether it is right to ordain women. Really? In our so-called enlightened land we are still torn as to whether women's contemplation of the divine carries with it the same legitimacy as men's? And we wonder why "none" is the fastest growing religious identity? Yet in our moral superiority, we think it somehow non sequitur that someone else might find it totally acceptable to take that same religiously and politically illegitimized woman and not just underpay her for equal work, but not pay her at all while forcing her to gratify his basest passions?

Here's the problem. We dignify this type of blatant preservation of unjustified privilege with our willingness to debate it. Gender equality isn't an unsettled matter. "We hold these truths to be self-evident that . . ." while Thomas Jefferson may have used gender-biased language, the issue of female equality is settled—and we need to stop deliberating it.

We should follow the example of Kenyan Nobel Peace Prize recipient Wangari Maathai who simply started planting thirty million trees in brazen protest of a dictator who was logging and land grabbing her homeland—particularly its women and children—into abject poverty. She just chose to defy the autocratic regime of the former Kenyan ruler Daniel arap Moi at every turn. When other women saw her courage, they joined her. Their efforts became known as the Green Belt Movement. Did those, mainly men, privileged under arap Moi's dictatorship rage

indignantly against them? Most certainly. According to Maathai's memoir, *Unbowed*, on December 12, in Uhuru Park during a speech celebrating independence from the British, President Moi suggested Maathai be a proper woman in the African tradition and respect men and be quiet.[5] Nonetheless, Maathai persevered, despite public slander, forced unemployment, unpardonable beatings, and baseless imprisonment. The power of her witness, however, is that she completely ignored arap Moi's

[5] Somehow oppressors nearly always carry the rage that is rightfully someone else's.

[6] Such would be one of only a handful of metaphors fully analogous to the fundamental truth of the incontestable equality of all.

repeated insistence of his privilege as being anything worthy of negotiation. She ignored him into extinction.

Not only do we often lend credibility where none resides with our incredible rehashing of ideas long spent, it seems to me we do another harm far more insidious. What happens to the mind taught to deny the light of day?[6] When we teach our children to embrace our prejudices—to argue for a thing that does not exist, long after the rationality of our argument has broken down—does that inhibit our children's ability to function rationally elsewhere? That is the thinking of which Anton Chekhov's protagonist in the short story "The Bet" spoke when he said:

> You have lost your reason and taken the wrong path. You have taken lies for truth, and hideousness for beauty. You would marvel if, owing to strange events of some sorts, frogs and lizards suddenly grew on apple and orange trees instead of fruit, or if roses began to smell like a sweating horse; so I marvel at you who exchange heaven for earth. I don't want to understand you.[7]

[7] Anton Chekhov, "The Bet."

"The Bet" is the story of two men, a banker and a lawyer, who had made a gentlemen's agreement for $2 million in the fervor of a dinner party debate over the morality of capital punishment that the lawyer could not survive fifteen years in solitary confinement. The years had passed and the day would come tomorrow that the lawyer would be free to collect his $2 million. The years had not been kind to the banker, and he did not have the money he had promised. The story opens with the banker contemplating murdering the lawyer in his sleep in order to avoid the certain scandal.

The banker sneaks into the guesthouse the lawyer has occupied for so long with nothing to keep him company but books and the creatures that would happen pass his windowsill. There he finds a note on the table beside the sleeping lawyer, now forty years old. The note, from which the previous quote was taken, chronicles all the lawyer has learned as a student and vicarious observer of humanity from his comfortable but lonely cell. He concludes his treatise with the astonishing turn: "To prove to you in action how I despise all that you live by, I renounce the two million of which I once dreamed as of paradise and which now I despise. To deprive myself of the right to the money I shall go out from here five minutes before the time fixed, and so break the compact . . ."

If Anton Chekhov could conceive of a way of being in the world that could refuse the privilege of which it once dreamed, if Zachaeus could refuse a privilege that he himself had earned, if Wangari Maathai could refuse to admit any credibility in a privilege for which others paid the price, couldn't we, too, refuse the privileges of inequity upon which so much of our society is built? In the case of gender equity in both so-called developed and developing countries, there are more women in the world than men. Furthermore, there are enough men who get it.[8]

[8] Even if there weren't, there are enough men still beholden to women in one way or another, which is relatively the same thing.

If the Zacchaeus story tells us anything, those of us who do get it could easily exploit the privilege we've given ourselves on behalf of those who are yet without and turn our societies completely around—if we really wanted to. Don't you think?

CHAPTER SEVEN

Ideas Concerning Plenty

On July 3, 2012 I received an email that read:

> According to the US Navy's own estimates, the use of high-frequency underwater sound for testing will deafen 15,900 whales and dolphins and kill 1,800 more over the next five years.

> Whales and dolphins depend on sound to navigate and live. The Navy is required to include comments from the public on their Environmental Impact Statement (EIS), so your signature and comment on my SignOn.org petition could help stop this naval program and save the lives of these ocean creatures.

> My petition says:

> Stop the killing of 1,800 whales and dolphins and the deafening of 15,900 more by ceasing the operation of the Navy's underwater sound system in the Hawaiian Islands, the California and Atlantic Coasts, and the Gulf of Mexico.

> Will you sign the petition? Click here to add your name, and then pass it along to your friends. Thanks for your help.

It was difficult for me to know where to put this. Just because human beings can do a thing doesn't mean we should. Technological fundamentalism is not an ethic that promotes life. Human life is inextricably intertwined with and interdependent upon all other forms of life on this planet in ways we have barely begun to understand.[1] The measure of collateral damage involved in this and other testing is no more acceptable among our fellow creatures than it would be if these were potential human casualties.

[1] Okay, except maybe for mosquitoes and roaches.

> "Man did not weave the web of life, he is merely a strand in it. Whatever he does to the web, he does to himself."
> ~Chief Si'ahl (Seattle), leader of the Dkhw'Duw'Absh (Duwamish) First Nations people

Plus, these estimates only relate to testing; they do not account for the degree of devastation caused by the regular use of the technology once testing is completed. We simply do not need any technology that costs this much—even if this Navy testing were the first step to an interactive-holographic-makes-it-appear-like-you're-sitting-in-the-same-room-talking-to-a-person mobile phone.

In a society that nixed the compostable Sun Chip® bag simply because we didn't like the sound of it, I don't hold out much hope for our fellow mammals, the whales.

"I Want" Is Too Small of a World for Us to Live In

My wife and I are constantly talking to our children about the importance of making room for each other. It's a really big deal for us, and a lesson we learned the hard way. Early in our marriage, Leslie and I feuded like the Hatfields and McCoys, jockeying for dominance, distrusting too much cooperation with the other. A lot of it was based on chasing someone else's dream for what life together should be like and mimicking others' failed scripts. We got to the point where we even distrusted the most sincere attempts at self-help just because the other had brought it to the table. Looking back now—twenty+ years in—all we can do is shake our heads and be thankful "God pities babies and fools," as the old folks used to say.

[2] New York: St. Martin's Press, 1997

One such time of costly distrust was when we had come across Stephen Covey's *7 Habits for Highly Effective Families.*[2] We both felt reading the book was an opportunity to create a family mission statement based on our most deeply held values. We went as far as to articulate a list of those values, assigned each

to its own sheet of paper and posted all twelve on the wall next to our bed in a giant circle. The idea was that during the next few weeks, as we walked by it, we would jot down on the pieces of paper specific ways of exemplifying the value printed on it. Yes, we succeeded . . . in sabotaging the whole thing. However, the one great thing that came out of our many laborious conversations is a phrase Leslie and I still use:

"I want" is too small a world for Us to live in.

It was the thing we just couldn't get right. We kept demanding that the other conform to the world we individually wanted, instead of making room for a world created together: for us, by us.

So we tell our children, "Make room for one another." But we don't just mean, "Be nice. Share your toys. Let her play too." Rather, it comes out of the deep intuition of shared ownership that potter Simon Levin (see chapter 5) had the audacity to advocate in interfaith dynamics. It also references the deep intuition of Enough (as in, "I have enough") articulated in the Sabbath economics work of people like American public theologian Ched Meyers. I figure that if my children learn the truth of abundance with their siblings, they can live it as a gift to the world.

However, there is a myth working against me, whose fallibility only came to my attention with the election of President Barack Obama. As a nation and as people of faith we believe in paying one's dues and waiting one's turn. It sounds as fair as fair can be—like everything we learned in kindergarten—the most useful presupposition in a meritocracy. So when Obama was elected and I was asked to contribute a chapter here and an article there, the question that kept raising itself with me was, "Is it finally black people's turn?" My initial hope was yes. But then I asked the question: Are there more beautiful ways of being in the world?

Real Leaders Lead

Consider the ideas of plenty set forth by David of Bethlehem's first three kingly acts.

David is a man slated to be king, but he has to wait sixteen years. In that sixteen years Saul, Israel's first king, tries to kill him several times, even though David is the champion of Israel and Saul's own son-in-law.

David is left with little alternative but to get off the grid. He goes into hiding in the wilderness.[3] People hear that he's out there and they get the idea that wherever David is must be a safe place. So they go to him, these men and women who've been exiled. Men and women who are regarded as criminals. Men and women who are categorized as socially unacceptable for one reason or another. Men and women who don't belong, according to society. They find refuge and safety together. Out in the wilderness, they build an egalitarian community together,

[3] See 1 Samuel.

one that looks much like the Israel that Yahweh had initially called them to.

And they do life together. They fight Saul together. They teach each other how to do justly and love mercy and walk humbly for better or worse. It's not an easy life to say the least; eventually they have to find refuge in a foreign land. Not just any foreign land, but the land of Israel's mortal enemies—the Philistines—to get far enough away where Saul can't threaten them anymore. Meanwhile, David has been anointed the next king of Israel.

Just long enough into their stay in Philistia that life has begun to take on a rhythm of normalcy, David receives an urgent message from the king of that land. "All able-bodied men are being summoned to defend Philistia's honor against those who want to destroy the Philistine way of life," he tells his people. With many reservations, the warriors of David eventually report for duty. Through an act of unanticipated providence, David and his men are thanked for their willingness to serve but are dismissed from service in the Philistine army because of suspicions about where their loyalties would lie in the heat of battle.

Gratitude for the asylum the Philistines offered was enough to make them fight to defend Philistia, but David and his men are grateful not to have to ride off to war against their brothers and sisters in Israel. As they ride back home at an easy pace, excited to share their good fortune with their wives and children, they are confused by what lies in the distance as they come over the ridge. There are a few straggling animals in the field, but no one attending them. Normally, there would be all sorts of hustle and bustle between the fields and the village. But today there is no one. A plow is hitched to an ass, yet no one is guiding it. What is going on?

They see the smoke. Something is wrong, terribly wrong. The closer they get the more pale they become. As Ziklag comes in full sight, all they can see are the charred ruins of their village. The Amalekites must have been spying on David's clan and seized the opportunity to raid as soon as the warriors had left.

As reality settles in on the band of intrepid soldiers, a great sorrow swells within them. They lift their collective voices and wail the heartache that only men of war know. Some fall to their knees and beat the ground. Others tear their clothes from their bodies. All seek as best they can to exhaust their grief and exorcise their guilt. Decisions need to be made and action taken that is not served by grief and guilt. The one sign of encouragement is the lack of bodies and blood. Their families have been kidnapped, not murdered. However, the kidnappers have a one- to three-day lead on them. They will have to be in pursuit soon.

Quickly their fighting spirit returns, so quickly that it seeks an immediate outlet. Some of the men blame their misfortune on David. He took them off to battle allied with Israel's enemies against their homeland. Rather than take their anger to heart, David directs that furious energy toward the real task at hand. He calls for Abiathar, a Levite, and asks him to retrieve the ephod used in prayer ceremonies, a breastplate traditionally worn by the chief priest since the time of Moses. David then prays with the ephod, as his ancestors had done. He asks God should he pursue those who had raided the village and would he overtake them. The answer comes back yes.

The best trackers among them determine which direction they need to travel. Those best at logistics begin to bark out orders about what supplies are needed and what can be off-loaded. The smiths check their sharpeners. The cooks, their flints and spices. When all is ready, the six hundred men get underway.

It is a flat-out sprint from their homes to Wadi Besor, a ravine about fifteen miles south—hard miles. Even with all the adrenaline coursing through their veins, the trip is four to six hours on foot. David is likely not the biggest guy or the strongest or the most skilled at everything, but he is undoubtedly the guy that won't stop, that can't give up—and many of his men are finding it hard to keep up with his pace. When they get to the ravine, a third of the men are too emotionally and physically exhausted to press on right away. It has to be the worst feeling in the world—to want to move, but the body simply says, "No."

David understands, but can't wait around. How can he camp while there is still daylight? With a blessing on those who have to rest, David and the others decide to lighten their load further. Leaving all except weapons and rations there on the north bank, David and four hundred men jump in chest-deep to wade across the chilly waters.

They continue, uncertain after a while whether they are still moving the right direction. What if they are off course? By a stroke of luck, they come across an Egyptian servant who had been left to die three days before, too ill to continue with his Amalekite master. David and his men feed the young man, who then points them in the right direction. After a battle that lasts a day and a half, David's warriors recover all they have lost, plus what the Amalekites had brought with them or stolen from others.

What David doesn't yet know is that he has become king of Israel by succession. Saul and three of his four sons had been killed in battle that day, and David was so far south of the assassinations that he was absolved of any suspicion. David is about to be king, but long before he had begun to cultivate the heart of a king true to Israel, a heart committed to the Sabbath ethic woven into the stories and rituals passed down from the time of Moses—myths that Israel has faith are inspired by God.

In his first act as king, David is challenged to deal with an issue of fairness raised by some of the four hundred men who put their lives on the line to recover those captured. The way the story has been handed down to us, the judgment of the Hebrew storytellers is that "the *corrupt* and *worthless* fellows among the men who had gone with David"[4] question why those who stayed behind with the bags should share in the spoils of victory with those who went all the way. Besides recovering their wives, sons and daughters, what part should the laggards have in the newly acquired wealth?

[4] 1 Samuel 30

David's response: "Those who stayed with the baggage will share in the wealth equally with those who fought." They shared in both hardship and promise over the years. This is not the time to parse whose contribution is worth more. This way of being is not just for those left standing on the Besor bank. It becomes a statute, an ordinance, for Israel that survives hundreds of years as the Hebrews tell and retell, affirm and re-affirm the story of their most revered king.

In his second act as a king, even before he knows he is king, David remembers those who have helped his band of outcasts in big and small ways over the years as they made an alternative life for themselves off-the-grid. This is the first time in more than five years that they have more than they need to sustain themselves. So David takes part of the cattle and produce and goods that the Amalekites have plundered from their raids beyond Ziklag and, before those who fought for them even get a share, he sends some back to their former benefactors as a token of appreciation.

On the third day after his return to Ziklag, news finally reaches David that Saul is dead, opening the way to make David the rightful king of Israel. As would be expected, people immediately try to ingratiate themselves by posturing themselves as forever in support of David. If only they knew the type of king David has already proven to be. The first sycophant to misjudge him is the messenger who brings word of the royal family's demise. Although his story isn't true, he intimates that he is the one who has in mercy ended the suffering of a mortally wounded King Saul (while at the same time being mindful that the opportunity for David's ascension had finally presented itself). So after supposedly disposing once and for all of the one who had driven David from his home and eventually from his country, this messenger brings David the crown and armlet of rulership.

David responds in his third recorded kingly act by having the messenger executed where he stands, for daring to raise his hand against Saul, "the Lord's anointed." Then David composes a song of lamentation to commemorate and mourn the loss of Saul, David's intermittently self-described enemy, and his son Jonathan, David's dear friend, both of whom he loves.

"That the People May Live"

Even within the egalitarian community David and his fellow refugees have built, as well as within the larger community of Israel and Judah who had known the myths of Jah's way all their lives, there remained mental structures of inequity. This is the thinking that somehow good can be fostered by marginalizing the weak or ignoring the community that supports you in your time of need (which all of us experience) or celebrating the misfortune of your enemies.

If nothing else, all three generate bad karma. For those who believe that our myths are not stories of what once happened, but rather, stories of what happens time and time again, all three represent seeds that have never yielded peaceable fruit. Beloved community requires someone who has a vision for a world in which there is plenty good room to step up and say, "I don't care what seems fair in that it puts us on top; we can see the failures of that way of being in the world through our own experiences. This is how we can live into something more beautiful."

David is remembered as the greatest king of Israel and a man after God's own heart. I believe this is why. When David caught a

[5] "In the Lakota culture," LaPointe informs us, "the young boy received his first name from something his father had seen or experienced. His adult name was given to acknowledge a noteworthy deed he accomplished in his adolescence or adulthood." Ernie LaPointe, *Sitting Bull: His Life and Legacy* (Layton, Utah: Gibbs Smith, 2009) 21.

[6] "In the Lakota culture, when a boy reached a certain age his father would approach either a brother or a brother-in-law. He would give this trusted man a gift and a filled pipe. Then the father would ask for his help in sharing with his son the Lakota way of being . . . Four Horns was the chief of the Bad Bow band of the Hunkpapa tribe, a man with deep wisdom and many honors. Jumping Badger was fortunate to have this uncle as his mentor" (Ibid., 22).

Just because human beings can do a thing doesn't mean we should.

glimpse of something better—more lovely, more just, more pure, more true, more beautiful—he sought to live it.

The more I understand about the Hebrew King David of Bethlehem, the more I see in him a particular kind of leadership that is often misidentified and misconstrued in Western culture. To hear Ernie LaPointe speak of his great-grandfather, Tatanka Iyotanka—commonly known by the English translation of his name, "Sitting Bull"—is to catch a glimpse of the same type of leadership in action.

In his book *Sitting Bull: His Life and Legacy*, LaPointe shares a story passed down by his mother about his great-grandfather's first buffalo hunt.[5] Before he had taken his adult name, he was called Jumping Badger:

> [Jumping Badger's uncle] Four Horns decided it was time to test his nephew's tracking and hunting skills.[6] The camp had moved closer to a big buffalo herd. While the rest of the hunters made preparations to go after the big herd, Four Horns took his nephew and told him to track a smaller heard farther to the west . . . . Four Horns advised jumping badger to be very careful, as this was his first hunt, and not to get caught in the center of the herd.

> Jumping Badger proceeded to ride right into the middle of the herd with his arrow fitted into the bow. He went after a big buffalo bull. His shot was true and he felled the big bull. The rest of the herd spooked and ran away, fortunately not trampling Jumping Badger in their panic.

> Four Horns was angry but also proud of his nephew. He asked Jumping Badger why he chose this particular big bull when there was a cow closer to the edge of the herd he could have taken. The boy replied that he had seen the cow but he also saw her calf. If he had taken the cow, her calf would surely have perished as well.

> The compassion of his young nephew amazed Four Horns. . . . Then Four Horns told the young boy to get his mother and relatives to help in preparing the meat.

> Jumping Badger rode fast to his mother's tipi and asked her to bring her sharp knives and all the relatives for the preparing of the meat. As she collected her skinning and

butchering tools, Jumping Badger gave his mother yet another reason to be proud of him. He took her outside and quietly indicated a nearby tipi where a widow lived with her two children. He told his mother to cut some of the choice portions of the meat and give them to the widow. Since she had no one to provide for herself and her children, this was his way of contributing to their welfare. Jumping Badger had just exhibited his compassion and generosity, and he was only ten years old.[7]

Non-Native American history books typically vilify or unfittingly venerate Sitting Bull as the great warrior, a Native American five-star general. But it was for the big-heartedness Tatanka Iyotake exhibited throughout his life that his own people venerated him. He was appointed by the people to be chief, primarily for his compassion, generosity, and humility, rather than for his undeniable skill on the battlefield.

Sitting Bull's magnanimous spirit found its fullest ceremonial expression in his participation in the Sun Dance. LaPointe explains the significance of the Sun Dance in conversation with Krista Tippett:

> See, most history books that are written about my grandfather said that he was a chief or medicine man, which he was, both. But through ceremony I was informed that he would like to be recognized as a Sun Dancer.[8]

> The Sun Dance [the Wiwang Wacipi] is one of the ceremonies that came with our sacred pipe. . . . The Sun Dance is about the survival of a culture, and you're doing this for the people. You don't do it for yourself. . . . You give your blood, sweat, tears, and you give all your energy [to the dance]. And everything you do out there is for the survival of the people, survival of the food sources, which is the four-legged: the buffalo, the deer, the antelope, whatever that you use to survive. . . . You do [the ceremony] to keep that going.[9]

Sitting Bull was our most humble, the most knowledgeable, spiritual man of his time. Those of us who practice, who live our religion, our spiritual way, we haven't even scratched the surface of what he knew and what he did with the sacrifices he did for his people. The compassion, the generosity he had for his people. . . . He would die

[7] Ibid., 24–25.

[8] "[Unedited] Ernie LaPointe with Krista Tippett," On Being with Krista Tippett, December 19, 2009, http://www.onbeing.org/program/ernie-lapointe-and-cedric-good-house-reimagining-sitting-bull-tatanka-iyotake/152.

[9] Ibid.

[10] Ibid.

for his people. And not only the people [the Lakota], but for every living thing on this earth. We're talking about Mother Earth and all living things on this earth. He prayed for their survival at the Sun Dance.[10]

Cedric Goodhouse, a member of Sitting Bull's band of the Lakota and part of a council of twelve that seeks to preserve the integrity of the Sun Dance echoes these thoughts as he tells how Tatanka Iyotake's legacy of making room for all survives in current efforts to heal from the devastation caused by the murder of Sitting Bull and the subsequent Massacre at Wounded Knee:

> The Sun Dance ceremony is so that the people may live. But prior to having [the Sun Dance as an annual ritual] out there on where Sitting Bull was killed, [we] had to have what they called Hunkapi ceremony, the Making a Relative ceremony, so that's what [we] did. We got together and we asked all the people that were associated or had any involvement in . . . that tragedy that occurred back in 1890, December 15th. And that means all the [Native American] police [who colluded with the US government to help subdue other natives], their descendants and relatives, and even the McLaughlins. . . .[11] We offered them all to come. [We Lakota were asked] to bring food and to bring clothing and to bring water, and we would make them relatives so that we can grow from that, you know, because it happened among our people. So that's what we did. We had this Hunkapi ceremony . . . before we could proceed on. . . . It was 25 years ago that we had this. . . .
>
> Today, there's a lot of things that we're going through . . . Governmentally-wise, if you come to Standing Rock, even here in Bismarck [where we are taping], you find things that are just are predominantly from that time. You see here in town Grant Marsh Bridge. We pass by Fort Lincoln. We pass by Custer's house. On Standing Rock, there's Fort Yates that's named after somebody. There's Fort Rice. . . . There's a town called Bull Head. There's a town called Little Eagle. There's a town called McLaughlin. It's just infested with that type of [anti-native culture] mindset yet. . . . There was a time where [native] people were even cheering on the Calvary when you went to the [picture] show, you know? Assimilation was

[11] The white US Indian Agent at Standing Rock reservation, James McLaughlin, who harbored no goodwill toward Sitting Bull, scheduled and organized the 25 December 1890 arrest of Sitting Bull in such a manner that it would most likely turn out badly.

that strong. . . . Even to today, there are still things people are saying . . . are okay, whereas the traditionalists would say, "No, that's not okay."

There was a lot of things we need to heal from and continue to, and it's happening. Bull Head, the people of Bull Head changed that name to Rock Creek, how that area used to be known in our language, "Rock Creek." And then the same way with Little Eagle. He was a[n accommodationist] policeman, but they changed that town's name to Running Antelope to honor the chief at that time. . . . And then . . . the Indian community of McLaughlin . . . changed [their part of McLaughlin to the name of] a man who owned the land in that area and he wanted to live in that area for trading purposes; his name was Bear Soldier. . . . In Fort Yates our community is now known as Long Soldier.

So there's a lot of things that have changed since that [first Making a Relative ceremony], and it's steadily [getting better]. And we're continuing to pray, you know, continuing to have the ceremony where we make relatives and continue to pray so that our people may live.[12]

Not Many People Are Smarter Than Neil deGrasse Tyson

I have a friend named Jimmy Chalmers. In many ways Jimmy and I are perceptually opposites. Jimmy sports a crew cut; I wear a ponytail. Jimmy has only a few strands of black hair remaining; I'm beginning to see a few strands of grey. Jimmy is an empty-nester. My wife and I are hostage for at least eight more years. If we have to claim political labels, which neither of us particularly like, Jimmy is a conservative, and I, a progressive who'd rather err on the side of social liberalism. And, oh yeah, Jimmy's a good ol' boy. Me, not so much.

Jimmy and I have so much more in common, including a shared commitment to an embodied faith and a family that serves as our primary attempt to leave the world better than we found it. Jimmy is the person who redeemed me from thinking conservatism was just another word for knee-jerk, self-absorbed tribalism. Jimmy says, "I'm conservative inasmuch as I'm a man who believes in founding documents." So he is a man of the Good Book and of

12 "[Unedited] Cedric Good House with Krista Tippett," On Being with Krista Tippett, December 19, 2009, http://www. onbeing.org/program/ ernie-lapointe-and-cedric-good-house-reimagining-sitting-bull-tatanka-iyotake/152.

the Constitution and of the best intuitions encapsulated therein. Disagree if you will, but one can't fault a man for that.

Jimmy graced Leslie and my dinner table one warm Atlanta summer evening. It was great to have him over. We talked work. We talked politics. We talked interests. But eventually our conversation came back around to that which matters to us most. I asked about his children. His oldest is out of the house and married. She and her husband are both brilliant. (As would be expected, she was homeschooled. What?)[13] They work in the Silicon Valley of the South on science-heavy projects that occasionally put them at lunch with astrophysicist and cosmologist Neil deGrasse Tyson, one of the smartest men in the world. Tyson is also an agnostic.

"So," Jimmy said, "they have laid down faith for the moment . . . but they'll be all right."

Now, Jimmy is a pastor. This is not how conservative Evangelical pastors talk. Thus, my response was only in part corroboration. It was mainly in an unnecessary attempt to comfort him that my mind formulated the response, "Perhaps it's the only way for God to save their faith."

The conversation continued in that vein for a little while, with me playing catch-up processing the big-heartedness I was hearing, while Jimmy articulated a most tender compassionate hope he maintains for his daughter and son (-in-law). I had heard this same compassion in him before, but it was directed at friends, not family. When it comes to our progeny, it's hard to maintain an even-keeled humble confidence. Desperation quickly seeps in. We want guarantees, assurances, results. But Jimmy, out of his evangelical experience, said, "I have to trust the Jesus in them."

I might not say it that way, but knowing (and sharing) much of the experience out of which Jimmy speaks, I have to praise the concession made in his words. It is no small thing to make room in one's thinking for more than just one possibility in the story of Jesus. All that went out the window when Christianity began to imagine itself besieged by science. Christianity never had any business trying to fight the science versus religion war; it was destined to lose. Science and religion ask and seek to answer two different sets of questions, substantiated by two different sets of proofs. And rather than doubling down and trying to win an empirical argument with his daughter on empirical grounds,

[13] Though a former classroom teacher, I'm a huge advocate for homeschool as the place where all children can thrive.

Jimmy said, "I have to trust." That type of broad-minded, big-hearted, deep-souled humility brings me to tears.

> There's always "plenty good room" for others.

All this—the stories of David and Sitting Bull as well as my experiences with my wife and kids and my friend Jimmy, even the politics of ecology and living in peace with our fellow creatures on this planet—stirs in me the intuition that making room for others leads to more room for ourselves to learn and grow and become more than our narrow sense of self once imagined possible.

I'm nearly convinced that the recognition that there is "plenty good room," as our ancestors used to sing, makes us most fully human.

> Plenty good room,
>
> Plenty good room,
>
> Plenty good room in my Father's kingdom.
>
> Plenty good room,
>
> Plenty good room,
>
> Choose your seat and sit down.[14]

[14] Negro spiritual

CHAPTER EIGHT

Inclinations Toward Liberation

If the previous three intuitions of beloved community[1] provide a lower threshold for those new to the conversation to begin grappling with how better faith stories give us better ways of showing up in the world, the last two we will consider will get us back to the world-changing we originally set out to do.

A lot has happened in the world since I started writing this book. For one thing, my poor MacBook keyboard's Q and W keys have gone out. There are only three ways for me to continue typing until I raise the money, do the research to locate what I need, and break down and buy a new keyboard to install or buy a new laptop altogether. One, I could only use words that have no Q's or W's. Two, I could instead utilize a little bluetooth keyboard I originally bought for my tablet.[2] Or three, I could depend on spell-check for all words that use the letter Q, while saving W on my clipboard and pasting it into the infinite number of common words that require W as I type.[3] Never mind that if I actually need to cut-and-paste a block of text, I have to remember to go back and save another lowercase W to my clipboard once I'm done. Yeah, it's an inconvenience, but what else can I do? I have to be able to write, right?

This experience of not having easy access to W's and Q's in a world of literacy that routinely requires them is quite analogous to my experience navigating Western society as a black man.[4] It's neither simple nor easy. But, as a middle-aged black man, I've learned to accommodate it. I was raising my children to do the same. But in the late summer of 2014 that all changed.

In the streets of a little town just outside St. Louis, Missouri, that no one, except those from the area, had any reason to know— Ferguson—a new consciousness about what it means to be black was born. That consciousness claimed as its mantra the Twitter

[1] Those intuitions being (1) Shared Ownership, (2) Leveraging Privilege on Behalf of Others, and (3) Making Room for Others.

[2] Which when people see, they tease me incessantly, "Why are you using a separate mini keyboard with your laptop?"

[3] Yes, that sentence required me to spell-check at least one word, paste in twelve W's, and then go back and cut-and-paste from a previous sentence however many capital Q's because it was just easier. But I've gotten used to it.

[4] LAWD! The stories I could tell just about getting this book published.

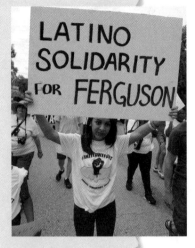

hashtag "#BlackLivesMatter"[5]—a pronouncement of dignity, a right to life, articulated for us by three courageous, young, gifted, black queer women: Patrisse Cullers, Alicia Garza and Opal Tometi.[6] It shook many of us awake who, after twenty or more years in adulthood, had become accustomed to accommodating our second-class plight.[7] The moment to which I refer is, of course, the protests that erupted in response to both the state-sanctioned murder of Michael Brown by Ferguson Police officer Darren Wilson and the conspiracy that ensued to obfuscate the circumstances surrounding Brown's impromptu execution and later justify it as a legitimate use of deadly force. This cycle of murder-obfuscation-justification repeated itself over and over in different locations across the country[8] in seemingly endless succession, and with each occurrence our resolve in the insistence of our own dignity grew.

From the beginning, ours was an inclusive resolve, folding into it the hopes and struggles of people of color and goodwill everywhere. It was always clear to those of us who embraced #BlackLivesMatter that it was a movement-building project of expanding solidarity and full inclusion. The only persons confused about that were those who chose to remain at a distance. As Todd "Speech" Thomas put it most succinctly in a TED Talk, "The reason we scream, 'Black Lives Matter!' is to make 'All lives matter' a true statement."[9] Since blackness is the extent to which equity in America has refused to go for four hundred years, we seek to stretch the blanket of justice so it can finally warm us all.

Ours was also a retrospective resolve, causing us to go back and rethink much of our understanding of ourselves as people of color over the last fifty years. One of the reevaluations that the young people at the forefront of this movement moment inspired was the need to interrogate the respectability politics in which so many of us had engaged in hopes of making social, economic, and political progress.[10]

Around the time my grandparents were born (early 1900s), folks would call the politics of respectability being "a credit to your race." One of my uncles (by friendship rather than blood) tells me that when he was growing up in rural Kentucky, just prior to the movement moment later named the civil rights era, his parents used to say to him, "If you behave respectably, you'll be respected." Though not quite as explicitly stated by time I was

[5] Originally coined in response to the July 2013 acquittal of George Zimmerman in the brutal murder of unarmed teen Trayvon Martin.

[6] #BlackGirlMagic. https://medium.com/@ patrissemariecullorsbrignac/ we-didn-t-start-a-movement-we-started-a-network-90f9b5717668#.3tistu8y7

[7] #StayWOKE!

[8] See pages 148-149 for partial list.

[9] TED Talk from "Speech," leader of the hip hop band Arrested Development, available at https://www.youtube.com/watch?v=bty-g1koxxg.

[10] Note how my own faith has evolved since writing chapter 3, where I said, "Respectability, and the pursuit thereof, is not a bad thing." That's the power of COMPOSTable faith stories. They keep us from becoming stagnant.

coming along,[11] the same "salvation by assimilation" sentiment was echoed in popular TV series like *Diff'rent Strokes*, *The Facts of Life,* and *The Cosby Show*, which touted paths to success out of reach for the vast majority of black people afflicted with the realities of the un- and underemployment, pervasive poverty, mass incarceration, or urban disinvestment of the Reagan years—often all four at the same time.

The Death of Dr. Cliff Huxtable

Our resolves got a little more complicated as #BlackLivesMatter moved from the streets of Ferguson to the streets of Staten Island to the streets of Baltimore. For one thing, we slowly began to realize that sunlight wasn't going to save us this time.[12] There was no overwhelming sense of shame or moral outrage for the unending succession of callous and brutal slayings of unarmed black and brown people by agents of the state as there had been for the public beatings in Selma and Birmingham fifty years prior. In fact, in most instances, the majority of outrage was directed at those who shined the light. The predominantly white perpetrators of state-sanctioned violence against black and brown bodies had gotten media savvy over the years. All they had to do was claim to have felt threatened, and all was forgiven by most who identified with them. It was as if folks predisposed toward empathy could only muster a cautious regret that couldn't help but believe there had to be some justification for each tragedy, despite what their eyes and ears told them.[13]

What was a little disconcerting is that *those who believe themselves white*, to borrow an expression from TaNehisi Coates,[14] publicly began to chastise protestors and activists with appeals to a caricature of Martin Luther King Jr. that became popular in the '80s—the peaceful accommodationist. Stricken from the record was the broad condemnation of King by their own parents and grandparents and, in many cases, themselves. Erased from their history texts was the memory of King as radical strategist, who bore proudly the labels of troublemaker, agitator, and "the most dangerous Negro" in America.[15] Sadly, the memories had even been wiped clean from some of the civil rights establishment[16] who, in affiliation with power over the past fifty years, had forgotten what it meant to protest for their lives. Thank God for folks like filmmaker Ava Duvernay, who gave us *Selma*, and the Movement for Black Lives coalition, who gave us #ReclaimMLK, for their valiant efforts to set the record straight.

[11] One of the favorite axioms of my day was, "You have to be twice as good to get half as far." But most of the time my mama was just like, "Act like you've got some sense!"

[12] The old folks used to say, "Sunlight is the best disinfectant."

[13] This is one of the observations that began to teach me that empathy is not the gateway to justice. It's the other way around. The Hebrew scriptures teach, "Do justly (know better, do better)," first. Then "love mercy (compassion), walk humbly (empathy)." I'm inclined to believe they are a progression.

[14] Coates is noting the intentionality behind the European invention and exportation of race, a construct that only serves to privilege some and un-/under-privilege others. For more read Ta-Nehisi Coates, Between the World and Me (New York: Spiegel & Grau, 2015).

[15] Quote from an August 30, 1963, FBI memo entitled "Communist Party, USA, Negro Question," written by William Sullivan, head of the Bureau's domestic intelligence division.

[16] Not to mention the whole activism cottage industry and nonprofit industrial complex that had grown up around the "right" (read "acceptable and dismissible") forms of protest and demonstration.

[17] A fact we see reflected in, among other things, both national parties' 2016 choices of presidential candidates, the refusal to let Obama pick a justice to succeed Scalia, and the resurgence of whiteness as the only acceptable medium for the conveyance of news.

[18] Read more about this and other political stereotypes foisted upon black women (and men) in the United States in Melissa Harris-Perry's *Sister Citizen* (Yale University Press, 2011). In the book's Introduction, she demonstrates how these stereotypes are marshaled against people of color, particularly in times of crisis.

[19] Before you take exception to my characterization of N.W.A., watch Ava Duvernay's 2008 documentary, *This Is the Life* to see all the mind-blowing hip hop talent coming out of Compton in the late '80s and then ask yourself how in the shadow of all that talent N.W.A. even got noticed.

[20] As professor Imani Perry notes in her interdisciplinary work *More Beautiful and More Terrible* (New York: New York University Press, 2011), "Racial narratives in the marketplace are also often commoditized. The products of the media version of racial narratives (television shows) bank upon a saleable image of ascriptive groups. The market winners of the sale of these images may be

Nonetheless, counter-narratives of "blame the victim" and "malign the protester" began to take shape—new iterations of all the old tropes. And it didn't matter that the Movement for Black Lives was undeterred by them. In the age of the twenty-four-hour opinion news cycle, the counter-narratives did their work inoculating the masses against the goals of disruption.[17] So when Toya Graham, who thinking of her child's safety in the moment and the risk the authorities posed to him, slapped her son upside the head for standing in solidarity with his friends in the Baltimore streets as the uprising began, those believing themselves white stepped to the mic as if with one voice and cheered, "Yes! Black Mammy![18] We thought you had gone from us! We need you to give us moral cover to put your unruly children back in their place." More than a few media outlets proclaimed Graham "[Old School] Mother of the Year" for reaffirming the natural order of things.

Then when, in carbon-copy timing to their injection into popular culture twenty-five years prior, N.W.A (Niggaz Wit Attitudes), the first hip hop artists to have broad cross-racial appeal, burst back into our consciousness with the release of *Straight Outta Compton*, that same populous breathed an audible collective sigh of relief, as if to communicate, "Those are the niggas we know and love!"[19] The supremacist logic seemed to go, "Black respectability—no problem. Black disrespect—we'll pay good money for that well-worn trope.[20] But young black and brown people in the streets demanding respect—now that's just a step too far!"[21]

Yet in an uncommon synchronicity of poetic justice, one of the most prominent purveyors of respectability, Bill Cosby, "America's Favorite Negro," um, I mean "Dad," and moralist to the masses, suffered his comeuppance. The actor/comedian/mogul, who in his 2004 "Pound Cake" speech had with the broadest of brushes painted poor black women as pathologically addicted to drugs and making babies,[22] had himself been giving black, brown, and white women drugs in order to practice making babies with them—all apparently against their will. In an amazing display of courage, thirty-five women came forward to tell their stories in a *New York* magazine article of how over the course of forty years Mr. Respectability had disrespected each of them in the most vile manner. All thirty-five sat for what has now become an iconic composite picture that included #TheEmptyChair. That empty chair has been filled now by more than fifteen other women—

and counting. When on December 30, 2015, Dr. William H. Cosby was formally indicted for rape, the young women and men who had first dared to cast off the oppressive adoration of "America's Favorite Dad" and the respectability he espoused were vindicated.

"Can't You Feel a Brand-New Day?"

In the wake of the acquittal of Trayvon Martin's murderer and the impromptu execution of Mike Brown, we had already begun to interrogate openly this notion that some people deserve justice and respect of their dignity, while others don't. Cosby's indictment was only wind in our sails. We questioned when exactly in history had respectability ever guaranteed respect for, let alone spared the life of, any persons of color.[23] The debate took place both publicly and privately, on news programs, and around kitchen tables. One such space of fair-minded critical examination was the Schomburg Center for Research in Black Culture in Harlem in New York.

In February 2016, Dr. Randall Kennedy, who had the previous October published an article in *Harper's* magazine arguing a progressive defense of respectability politics, was invited to debate Dr. Brittney Cooper and Mychal Denzel Smith on the merits of our continued reliance on respectability as a useful construct for collective advancement and achievement. Kennedy issued a strong affirmative argument in favor of respectability, followed by a brilliantly incisive rebuttal by Cooper, to which Kennedy gave a somewhat redundant response, insisting that respectability had produced a progress that was otherwise unattainable. Mychal Denzel Smith then articulated a core critique of respectability in the most concise and poignant terms I have ever heard marshaled in explanation of what is new in this moment: "You can stick with progress [if you want to]. We want liberation!"

Some Things Never Change

A little under two thousand years ago, a quite different, yet remarkably similar, debate about a particular less-than-respectable woman began in Palestine. For the sake of argument, let's call the courageous woman at the center of the debate Maria.

of any color. We should be careful not to assume because the images may be sold or profited from by a member of a disfavored ascriptive group that they are not racist."

[21] "The trigger for white rage, inevitably, is black advancement. It is not the mere presence of black people that is the problem; rather, it is blackness with ambition, with drive, with purpose, with aspirations, and with demands for full and equal citizenship. It is blackness that refuses to accept subjugation, to give up," noted Carol Anderson, *White Rage: The Unspoken Truth of Our Racial Divide* (New York: Bloomsbury, 2016).

[22] Melissa Harris Perry, *Sister Citizen* (New Haven, CT: Yale University Press, 2011), is again helpful in articulating just how politically consequential such pronouncements are. "Welfare policy is intimately linked in the American imagination with black women's sexuality. Political scientist Martin Gilens [and Ange-Marie Hancock show] that white American opposition

> "Freedom is always coming in the hereafter. . . . The hereafter is a hustle. We want it now."
> ~Jesse Williams, at the 2016 BET Awards

to welfare results from whites' fixed beliefs that the system supports unworthy black people who lack a suitable work ethic."

[23] It didn't for Martin Luther King Jr, Medgar Evers, or el-Hajj Malik el-Shabazz (Malcolm X)—arguably the most respectable among us.

[24] This is the second publication in which I've used this political campaign trope. I owe it to the creativity and research of my friend Brian McLaren.

[25] Yeah, sounds like the ticket and privatized probation racket in Ferguson and many other US cities.

A high society party was being hosted at the home of Simon, a prominent member of the Jewish Pharisee religio-political party.[24] While the socialite scene had become a bore, when Maria heard who the guest of honor would be, she had to be there. She had been following the Galilean's messianic campaign for months. He and popular political dissident, Barabbas (and others to a lesser degree), had been holding rallies, both drawing big crowds. A good many of the Pharisees had already written this Jesus character off, but not all; hence, the party. But Maria's mind was already made up. She and many others who felt like outsiders saw in Jesus someone they could rally behind. The insiders and strivers couldn't see what they saw in him, or didn't want to. Maria believed Jesus was someone who wasn't going to rise to prominence and forget the promises he'd made about justice and liberation.

The way the story is told Maria is described as "a sinner." Nowadays that language has little currency outside of church, and even in church, it's like describing someone as human. Church folk say "All have sinned." So "sinner" is basically a catchall term for being on the wrong side of God (as if humans get to make that determination), usually referring to folks who are wrong and know it. As my mama used to say, "At least they committed to sump'in." However, in first-century Palestine, the label *sinner* had social, economic, and even political implications.

As first-century Jews, sinners were expected to atone for their sins. That meant going to the Temple and buying the requisite peace offering, which varied based on your income bracket, while avoiding being swindled by the money changers and merchants. Many of these vendors had a kickback racket going with key Temple priests. Merchants would switch the animal you thought you were buying as atonement for one with a blemish that wouldn't pass inspection by the priest. The priest would then reject the offering, requiring you to pay a fine (the equivalent of forty days' wages) for bringing a blemished offering "to the Lord".[25] Of course, for most people this meant being in debt to the Temple for long periods of time and paying whatever interest was associated with that. Then, the priests and merchants in on the scam (or the money changers and wealthy landowners who had their own scams run through the Temple[26]) would split the proceeds. Like I said, a racket! If you were too poor to pay-to-play, then you were shunned by members of the community in good standing. If you were male, you also ran the risk of losing the right to speak in the assembly when communal decisions were being made.

Why must we assume that a woman's sin must be sexual? We never make that assumption of a man.

As a woman, Maria didn't have to worry about that last part. However, communal standing had its benefits. The thing is we don't know what her sin was. Herein is yet another place where debate lies. Traditionally, this woman we are calling Maria is thought of as a whore, a prostitute, a lady of the night, but there is no real basis for that, except she had a little money, and she isn't remembered as being attached to a man. (So she must be a prostitute, right?) There's also the rumor that she was the Mary from Magdala (Mary Magdalene) who had seven demons cast out of her;[27] however, there's little evidence of that either. "Sinner" could have also meant liar, cheat, or murderer. Or it could have just meant unmarried adult woman, person of mixed ethnicity, free-thinker or one who owed a Temple debt—like I said, *outsider*. The fact that being an unmarried, free-thinking adult woman of mixed heritage who owed money to the Temple could be seen in the same light as being a murderer says a lot about how oppressive the insider regime had become to outsiders.

These outsiders were the early supporters of the Jesus campaign. Folks whom the major Pharisee and Sadducee religio-political parties dismissed. Folks who were too plugged into the system for the Essenes who were committed to living off the grid. Folks who were too timid for the Zealots who were trying to provoke an all-out civil war. Folks not shrewd and cutthroat enough for the Herodians and their house of cards. All these different factions talked a good game about liberating Jews from Roman supremacy, but Jesus seemed to be the only one working to do something long-term about it.

Maria had to be there to connect with Jesus, to let him know he had her backing. She wanted to be a part of the world he imagined possible—where outsiders would become insiders and the whole concept of outside/inside would be blown up. Whatever privilege she may have had, despite her sinfulness, she wasn't invested in it. So she got dressed and left, taking with her a campaign contribution.

When she got to the party, she congregated with the women as was the custom, but she kept looking Jesus's direction. Something

[26] For money changers, even today, the racket is always about exchange rates. Inconsistency always helps to increase profit, because the person you are dealing with never knows what's fair or not. While priests maintained the rules that all Roman money had to be exchanged for Jewish coin before it entered the Temple, the money changers made a killing on their captive audience and split the profits with their priestly benefactors. What a lot of people don't know is that first-century Jewish priests under Roman occupation weren't just religious leaders; they were also the judges for local small claims proceedings. So some had a similar scam with absentee landowners in which they would consistently rule in landowners' favor in exchange for payoff, when peasant tenants brought charges of neglect, harassment or damages. This insight is based on the work of public theologian Ched Myers. More can be found in his seminal commentary on the Gospel of Mark, *Binding the Strong Man* (Maryknoll, NY: Orbis, 1988, 2008).

[27] Perhaps actual demons or maybe just a euphemism for mental illness.

wasn't right. Maybe it was the minimal number of real Jesus supporters in the room. Not that anyone was openly hostile, but she knew this crowd. They were being phony and she couldn't stand it. Or maybe it was the chumminess of the host—working the room, sucking up to Jesus's disciples, trying to peddle a little influence. Or maybe it just felt all too familiar, the same old insiders' game of maintaining a status quo that had already cost too many outsiders their lives. Whatever it was, Maria started to weep uncontrollably, and in good African tradition,[28] the other women of the community instinctively looked to step into their roles of either joining in the grief or praying or remedying the problem or going to inform family members, whatever it might be. However, looking around, it didn't take long to notice no one was hurt.

[28] Because you know all this is happening in North Africa, right?

It was a clever way to get everyone's attention, but not just that. Now that she had it, Maria wanted to do something with it. For so long her people had looked for the one who could help them make a change that could make a difference. So many times they had been disappointed when this or that candidate for Messiah had turned out to be ineffectual or just in it for personal gain. So easy it had become just to play the role that best fit one's personality, whether colluder with empire or assimilationist or accommodationist or religionist or activist or community organizer or protester or person who didn't give a damn—none of which necessarily brought liberation. Consumed with the momentary sense that all was pointless, Maria took out her campaign contribution and almost threw it to the floor, where it would have shattered and been lost.

On second thought, Maria let down her hair (a gesture of defiance for a woman in those days) and, opening the alabaster vial in hand, marched to where Jesus was lounging in conversation, his feet curled behind him. She dropped to her knees, pouring the sweet, expensive oil from the ornately carved vial and with it and her tears she washed, as it were, the feet of Jesus, sopping up the excess with her hair. I imagine that, in between sobs and blowing kisses at his feet,[29] she blurted out the only thing she knew for sure would focus Jesus's attention in the direction she wanted:

[29] I refuse to believe she put her lips to his grimy toes; I don't care who he was!

How lovely on the mountains

 Are the feet of him who brings good news,

Who announces peace

And brings good news of happiness,

Who [proclaims] salvation,

And says to Zion, "Your God reigns!"[30]

[30] Isaiah 52:7 NASB.

As if to say, "Don't forget why you are here, why we love you, why we will follow you wherever you lead. Who cares if the other folks don't get it, if they think I'm trying to come on to you? I need *you* to get it!"

It seems right that Maria would have chosen a poem from Third Isaiah, considering Jesus had repeatedly described his campaign in terms of the school of Isaiah's whole release-the-oppressed, set-the-captives-free tagline. Jesus obviously saw the connection between her actions and Third Isaiah's message, because he responds to Simon's side-eye with a quick aside about two debtors whose debts had been cancelled: one who owed five hundred days' wages; the other owed fifty.

Jesus then asked, "Which of the two would be most appreciative?"

Simon responded, "I suppose the one who had been forgiven the most."

To which Jesus replies, "Exactly. Open your eyes. See this woman for the gift she is. Without her, you'd be clueless. I came to your house as a candidate for Messiah, and you didn't even think enough of me to offer me water for my feet, no kiss of friendship, no blessing oil. This wonderful woman, on the other hand, who unjust custom puts outside the room, cared enough about what might not be right about this whole thing to risk coming into this space to grab my attention and remind me of my obligations. That's love. That's why she is released of her debts today— literally, not just spiritually—though they are many. You don't get it, because you don't know what it's like to risk it all for something better. Life for you is already pretty good."

Jesus then realized that he'd been talking to Simon all that time. Shaking his head, he turned to Maria and said, "Sister, don't worry about these people. You're free. This is what discipleship looks like. Thank you."

[31] Many thanks to Luke scholar Bridgett Greene for helping me find Maria's voice in this story.

And the folks standing around watching the scene unfold looked at each other, wondering out loud, "He can do that?"[31]

32 If you are unfamiliar with womanist scholarship, check out the documentary *Journey to Liberation: The Legacy of Womanist Theology*, by the late filmmaker Anika Gibbons.

#SayHerName

Having read this book up to this point, you hopefully feel that parts of this story are a bit shady, maybe even more so if you know the traditional telling. To quote womanist theologian[32] Renita Weems,

> There is no denying that a significant part of our work . . . is to radically rethink what it means to continue to [tell] certain kinds of obnoxious, oppressive stories in the Bible where women's rape and abuse and marginalization are romanticized, subjugated, and excused for the sake of some alleged larger purpose in the story. Stories like . . . the prostitute who anoints Jesus's feet with her tears and hair in Luke 7 [is one] we cannot afford to continue reading without serious rethinking. Their story of women's abuse and subjugation may be too costly to hold on to [sic] and too hopelessly misogynistic to try saving.[33]

33 "Re-Reading for Liberation," chapter 4 of *Womanist Theological Ethics: A Reader,* ed. Katie Geneva Cannon, Emilie Maureen Townes, and Angela D. Sims (Louisville: Westminster John Knox, 2011). The whole book is a must read.

Honestly, I'd rather let the story go. This whole debate about the one we've called Maria being a prostitute, just because she uses her agency and her money as she pleases and this trying to erase her identity or conflate it with others makes me want to puke. The only reason I tell it is the need to correct the wrongs perpetrated by the traditional telling of it. As we discussed in chapter 3, persons in power-over positions can't just skip to the good part once they realize their mistakes. Yes, we have to learn to listen. We also have, as far as is possible, to make amends. As a man, this story helps me to name some of the amends I need to make.

34 Who the hell were we reading in college if not womanist and liberation authors?

I have learned so much in the past few years about how heteropatriarchy works that I wish I had known at the beginning of adulthood.[34] The ways that women and queer persons—particularly women and queer persons of color—get over-talked or boxed out of conversations. Have their ideas minimized, then stolen. Get invited into things at the last minute. Suffer the indignity of having everything framed in male or heterosexually normative terms. Have the risks they take (opportunities they pursue) second-guessed. Have their autonomy/self-determination limited. Are overmanaged, denied funding, and so on. For too long these injustices were easy to ignore or excuse.

My sincerest thanks to all those who have challenged and, at the same time, borne long with me—particularly my wife—as I've sought to grow.

Honestly, the way the story has been handed down to us feels too much like a patriarchal domination fantasy, if not outright misogyny, this notion of a female prostitute fawning at the feet of a man with all its sensationalizing hyper-eroticism. Even if we hold that it was a different time and a different culture, we still have to wrestle with the unwarranted sexualization of the story. Why must we assume that a woman's sin must be sexual? We never make that assumption of a man. We also have to wrestle with the erasure of the protagonist's name. What does it mean to render women invisible, even as their stories remain authoritative in our lives? Do we really believe that's accidental? We even have to wrestle with the historical conflation of this woman's story with the stories of Mary of Bethany (Martha and Lazarus's sister) and Mary Magdalene (the first witness to Jesus's resurrection). Do we really think it is by chance that the nearly twelve female disciples mentioned by name in the Jesus story get conflated down to about six, in contrast to the twelve men whose names we are taught to memorize in church growing up? No wonder our world is rife with patriarchy and misogyny! The one place that should have taught us differently actually gave us the most ironclad means and rationale to despise women, to convince many to accept it and to feel obligated to pass that way of being in the world on to their children.

So here's how this story and others like it warp both our faith and the world. In rehearsing this story in its traditional form, women become expendable, like Sandra Bland hanging in a Texas jail cell. In repeating this story in its traditional form, women become props in a recurrently violent narrative masquerading as innocent, as was the nature of the story told by MSNBC regarding Melissa Harris Perry, whose news show became a target for preempting by network executives for being too progressive on gender, race, and social justice. In reiterating this one story in its traditional form, women serve only our erotic desires, as so many expected Beyoncé to do instead of her calling women of color into "Formation." In reciting this story in its traditional form, women are placed in the background as if secondary or only in service to the real story, much like Delores Huerta, who co-founded United Farm Workers with Cesar Chavez

> "And I cried... for all of the women who stretched their bodies for civilizations, only to find ruins."
> ~Sonia Sanchez, poet

and was the one of the two who actually stayed true to its mission. In regurgitating this story in its traditional form over and over, women's contributions are minimized, much like the contributions of Helen Zia, a profoundly impactful journalist, writer, and activist, who like so many women of Asian-Pacific Islander (API) descent I had never heard of until an Asian-American friend who co-wrote the study guide for *BETTER* mentioned her to me. And that's just this one story. With each traditional telling of it, these violations are justified down in the core of our being, then replicated by us time and again in the world.

> We don't just need to reform our views and the systems and structures we've built to institutionalize them; we need to transform them.

The intuition that arises for me out of this story is that we don't just need to reform our views and the systems and structures we've built to institutionalize them; we need to transform them. This takes me back not just to the COMPOST attributes, but also to the COMPOST process itself:

1. Read the passage for what it says and doesn't say. *In this case, Luke 7.*

2. How have you traditionally heard this story told? *I share that at length above. If you have no traditional interpretation to deconstruct, count yourself lucky!*

3. List three things you love about the passage as you are now reading it. *They all show up in the story. For me, it was Maria's self-determination, her wisdom in understanding why Jesus is worthy of her backing, and her willingness to put her money and reputation at risk—something Simon and others just didn't get. Bonus, I like that Jesus eventually stops talking to Simon and gives his attention and affirmation fully to Maria.*

4. List three things that bug you about the story itself or about the way the story is typically recounted. *(I do that at length directly above.)*

5. Articulate three questions that come to mind when you think of this story. *What was the nature of Maria's relationship to those who gathered at the party? What was her sin? What was symbolic and significant about the whole perfume and kisses and tears and hair on the feet that we just wouldn't understand today?*

6. Now, select at least one thing from each of the three preceding categories and use them to reimagine the

story, keeping in mind the seven attributes of stories that COMPOST.

Yes, stories that COMPOST attempt transformation by recognizing that the best part of the tradition is the acknowledgment that our understanding of the story of God is never complete, but also by moving us through a way of approaching our sacred myths that ask us to consider them from multiple vantage points.[35] As we grow, our understanding of what is beautiful, just, and virtue-filled should grow. That does mean that some things we will only come to know and be able to practice over time.

But, we don't get two thousand years to get it right.

Celebrate Recovery, Not Addiction

We can do better—right now—pure and simple.

In my day job as a design-based collaborative problem-solver,[36] I often talk about the pursuit of beloved community, because the biggest problems the communities of goodwill I work with tend to have are ones they create for themselves around others' social identities (race, gender, sexual orientation, gender expression, faith, and so on). The work we do together involves either building the equity, diversity, or inclusion necessary for an organization to move toward beloved community or maintaining the equity, diversity, or inclusion they've built as they solve for other problems.

I often describe beloved community as more of a twelve-step program than a semester-length seminar. You can know all the right stuff and never get around to practicing it. Recently a Facebook friend responded to a post I made about MSNBC's attempt to make the MHP Show—the best news analysis (not just talk) show on television—vanish from before our eyes. He said:

> The other day, I saw Calvin Hill (NFL legend and father of NBA great Grant Hill) call himself 'a recovering sexist' and liken it to an addiction, and I think that was a really helpful perspective for me.

> We're addicted to social power and we're addicted to the narcissistic pleasure we get from wielding that power. But then if we're not even willing to admit it, how can we claim to be in recovery?

[35] Here's my twenty years as a teacher coming out of me, because I know how valuable practice can be. It would be a relatively simple matter for you to do this same analysis on each of the other seven stories in the book, then turn around and start telling your own better faith stories.

[36] http://collabyrinthconsulting.com.

A 12-step program… describes pretty well what the moment was like for me. Here [Hill] was an extremely brilliant and accomplished black man who seemingly had nothing to explain to anyone, and yet he was modeling for me the kind of confession I most needed to make. That moment of "Yes, absolutely yes, I need to say those words, understand those words, and say them again, because I want to be more like this man."

He was saying them about sexism, but I needed to say them about both [sexism and racism]. I sat there playing back the video over and over on Hulu, while I wrote it all down because I wanted to get them just right, because I think I was also beginning to realize that from my position, I have to be a listener, a learner, a receiver of wisdom. That my own words aren't strong enough to help me understand racism, because my perspective has been so limited (intentionally limited, really. Self-medication by creative cultural fiction). I needed truth from someone who hasn't been sheltered from it.

> We also have, as far as is possible, to make amends.

I couldn't agree more, which is why I'm convinced the only ones who can lead us out of this cycle of circular reform masquerading as progress are the very women of color and queer persons of color we've spent thousands of years erasing from our faith stories.

Transformation and liberation lie in being able to recognize that it is time for the last to be first, as Jesus once said, and then to figure out what role the rest of us are going to play in helping to "make all things new." Whites, men, heterosexuals, traditionally able-bodied persons no longer have to dominate the leading roles onstage or offstage. It takes a lot of different people to bring a top-notch production to the screen or stage. You have various different kinds of producers, you have researchers, publicists, marketers, promoters, agents, talent scouts, location scouts, stage/set manager, grips, runners, costume designers, lighting, sound, set designers, props manager, band members, venue manager, concessions manager, advocates, audience—the list is almost infinite. My joy and challenge of late has been in trying to figure out the various roles I can play to help bring about the liberation I too long to feel.[37]

37 "I Wish I Knew How It Would Feel to Be Free," Nina Simone.

Rest In Power

Alfred Olango, 30, CA—killed 27 Sept 2016

Tawon Boyd, 21, MD—17 Sept 2016

Terence Crutcher, 40, OK—16 Sept 2016

Levonia Riggins, 22, FL—30 Aug 2016

Alfred Toe, 34, NJ—27 Aug 2016

Jorge Ceniceros, 22, AR—19 Aug 2016

Silivenusi Ravono, 46, CA—18 Aug 2016

Marcos Gastelum, 24, AR—16 Aug 2016

Kendrick Brown, 18, AK—13 Aug 2016

Fred Barlow, 61, CA— 9 Aug 2016

Richard Swihart, 32, CA—1 Aug 2016

Manuel Dela Cruz, 26, TX—1 Aug 2016

Paul O'Neal, 18, IL—28 Jul 2016

Donnell Thompson Jr, 27, CA—28 Jul 2016

Dalvin Hollins, 19, AR—27 Jul 2016

Humberto Martinez, 32—26 Jul 2016

Andrew Esquivel, 21—17 Jul 2016

Delrawn Small, 37—4 Jul 2016

Fermin Valenzuela, 32—2 Jul 2016

Rodrigo Guardiola, 36—25 Jun 2016

Deravis "Caine" Rogers, 22—23 Jun 2016

Pedro Cruz-Amado, 24—21 Jun 2016

Clarence Howard, 25—19 Jun 2016

Antwun Shumpert, 37—18 Jun 2016

Omar Villagomez, 21—7 Jun 2016

Ollie Brooks, 64—28 May 2016

Ernesto Carraman, 41—28 May 2016

Devonte Gates, 21—26 May 2016

Doll Pierre-Louis, 24—25 May 2016

Vernell Bing Jr, 22—22 May 2016

Michael Wilson Jr, 27—22 May 2016

Jessica Williams, 29—19 May 2016

Jermias Cruz, 30—19 May 2016

Mylynda Martinez, 27—13 May 2016

Ashtian Barnes, 25—28 Apr 2016

Terrill Thomas, 38—24 Apr 2016

Willie Tillman, 33—23 Apr 2016

Demarcus Semer, 21—23 Apr 2016

Kevin Hicks, 44—5 Apr 2016

Darius Robinson, 41—4 Apr 2016

Torrey Robinson, 35—19 Mar 2016

Richard Gonzalez, 55—16 Mar 2016

Cristian Medina, 23—16 Mar 2016

Jose Cruz, 16—13 Mar 2016

Peter Gaines, 35—12 Mar 2016

Marco Loud, 20—12 Mar 2016

Daniel Chavez, 41—7 Mar 2016

Abelino Cordova-Cuevas, 28—7 Mar 2016

Christopher Davis, 21—24 Feb 2016

Inocencio Cardenas Jr, 38—15 Feb 2016

Dyzhawn Perkins, 19—13 Feb 2016

Calin Roquemore, 24—13 Feb 2016

Gustavo Najera, 22—9 Feb 2016

David Joseph, 17—8 Feb 2016

Wendell Celestine Jr, 37—5 Feb 2016

Antronie Scott, 36—4 Feb 2016

Randy Nelson, 49—3 Feb 2016

Joseph Molinaro, 34—2 Feb 2016

Filberto Valencia, 26—19 Jan 2016

Keith Childress, Las Vegas, NV
—killed 31 Dec 2015

Bettie Jones, Chicago, IL—25 Dec 2015

Kevin Matthews, Dearborn, MI—23 Dec 2015

Leroy Browning, 30, Palmdale, CA
—20 Dec 2015

Roy Nelson, Hayward, CA—19 Dec 2015

Miguel Espinal, 36, Yonkers, NY—8 Dec 2015

Nathaniel Pickett, 29, Barstow, CA
—19 Nov 2015

Tiara Thomas, Portage, IN—18 Nov 2015

Cornelius Brown, Opa-locka, FL
—18 Nov 2015

Chandra Weaver, 48, Kansas City, MO
—17 Nov 2015

Jamar Clark, Minneapolis, MN—15 Nov 2015

Richard Perkins, 39, Oakland, CA
—15 Nov 2015

Stephen Tooson, 45, Birmingham, AL
—12 Nov 2015

Michael Lee Marshall, 50, Denver, CO
—11 Nov 2015

Alonzo Smith, 27, Washington, DC
—1 Nov 2015

Yvens Seide, 33, Big Cypress, FL
—31 Oct 2015

Anthony Ashford, 29, San Diego, CA
—27 Oct 2015

Lamontez Jones, 39, San Diego, CA
—20 Oct 2015

Rayshaun Cole, 30, Chula Vista, CA
—17 Oct 2015

This is a partial list of more than 200 unarmed persons of color killed by police or under suspicious circumstances in police custody since I began writing this book.

"Here, in this here place, we flesh; flesh that weeps, laughs; flesh that dances on bare feet in grass. Love it. Love it hard. Yonder they do not love your flesh. They despise it. They don't love your eyes; they'd just as soon pick em out. No more do they love the skin on your back. Yonder they flay it."

"And O my people they do not love your hands. Those they only use, tie, bind, chop off and leave empty. Love your hands! Love them. Raise them up and kiss them. Touch others with them, pat them together, stroke them on your face 'cause they don't love that either. You got to love it, you! And no, they ain't in love with your mouth. Yonder, out there, they will see it broken and break it again. What you say out of it they will not heed. What you scream from it they do not hear. What you put into it to nourish your body they will snatch away and give you leavins instead. No, they don't love your mouth. You got to love it."

Paterson Brown, 18, Richmond, VA —17 Oct 2015

Christopher Kimble, 22, East Cleveland, OH —3 Oct 2015

Junior Prosper, North Miami, FL —28 Sept 2015

Keith McLeod, 19, Reisterstown, MD —23 Sept 2015

Wayne Wheeler, 44, Lathrop, MI—7 Sept 2015

India Kager, Virginia Beach, VA—5 Sept 2015

Tyree Crawford, Newark, NJ—1 Sept 2015

James Carney III, 48, Cincinnati, OH —31 Aug 2015

Felix Kumi, 61, New York, NY—28 Aug 2015

Wendell Hall, 50, Kansas City, KS —27 Aug 2015

Asshams Manley, 30, Spauldings, MD —14 Aug 2015

Christian Taylor, 19, Arlington, TX —7 Aug 2015

Troy Robinson, 32, Decatur, GA—6 Aug 2015

Brian Day, Las Vegas, NV—25 Jul 2015

Michael Sabbie, Texarkana, TX—22 Jul 2015

Billy Ray Davis, Houston, TX—20 Jul 2015

Samuel Dubose, Cincinnati, OH—19 Jul 2015

Darrius Stewart, Memphis, TN—17 Jul 2015

Albert Davis, 23, Orlando, FL—17 Jul 2015

Sandra Bland, 28, Waller County, TX —13 Jul 2015

Salvado Ellswood, 36, Plantation, FL —12 Jul 2015

George Mann, 35, Stonewall, GA —11 Jul 2015

Jonathan Sanders, 39, Stonewall, MS —8 Jul 2015

Victo Larosa III, Jacksonville, FL—2 Jul 2015

Kevin Judson, 24, McMinnville, OR —1 Jul 2015

Spencer McCain, Owings Mills, MD —25 Jun 2015

Kevin Bajoie, 31, Baton Rouge, LA —20 Jun 2015

Zamiel Crawford, 21, McAllah, AL —20 Jun 2015

Jermaine Benjamin, 42, Vero Beach, FL —16 Jun 2015

Kris Jackson, 22, South Lake Tahoe, CA —15 Jun 2015

Alan Craig Williams, Greenville, SC —13 Jun 2015

Ross Anthony, Dallas, TX—9 Jun 2015

Richard Gregory Davis, Rochester, NY —31 May 2015

Markus Clark, Fort Lauderdale, FL —21 May 2015

Lorenzo Hayes, Spokane, WA—13 May 2015

De'Angelo Stallworth, Jacksonville, FL —12 May 2015

Dajuan Graham, Silver Spring, MD —12 May 2015

Brandon Glenn, Los Angeles, CA —6 May 2015

Reginald Moore, Greenville, MS—6 May 2015

Nuwnah Laroche, Ridgefield Park, NJ —6 May 2015

Jason Champion, Ridgefield Park, NJ —6 May 2015

Bryan Overstreet, 30, Sylvester, GA —28 Apr 2015

Terrance Kellom, 20, Detroit, MI—27 Apr 2015

David Felix, New York, NY—25 Apr 2015

Lashonda Ruth Belk, 25, West End, NC —24 Apr 2015

Gregory Daquan Harris, 25, West End, NC —24 Apr 2015

Terry Lee Chatman, Houston, TX —23 Apr 2015

William Chapman, Portsmouth, VA —22 Apr 2015

Samuel Harrell, 30, Beacon, NY—21 Apr 2015

Freddie Gray, Baltimore, MD—19 Apr 2015

Norman Cooper, San Antonio, TX —19 Apr 2015

Brian Acton, Columbia, TN—18 Apr 2015

Darrell Brown, Hagerstown, MD—17 Apr 2015

Frank Shephard III, 41, Houston, TX —15 Apr 2015

Walter Scott, North Charleston, SC —4 Apr 2015

Donald "Dontay" Ivy, Albany, NY—2 Apr 2015

Eric Harris, 73, Tulsa, OK—2 Apr 2015

Phillip White, Vineland, NJ—31 Mar 2015

Dominick Wise, 30, Culpeper, VA —30 Mar 2015

Jason Moland, Ceres, CA—29 Mar 2015

Nicholas Thomas, Atlanta, GA—24 Mar 2015

Denzel Brown, 21, Bayshore, NY —22 Mar 2015

Brandon Jones, Cleveland, OH—19 Mar 2015

Askari Roberts, 35, Rome, GA—17 Mar 2015

Terrance Moxley, Mansfield, OH
—10 Mar 2015

Anthony Hill, Chamblee, GA—9 Mar 2015

Bernard Moore, Atlanta, GA—6 Mar 2015

Naeschylus Vinzant, Aurora, CO—6 Mar 2015

Tony Robinson, Madison, WI—6 Mar 2015

Charly Leundeu "Africa" Keunang,
Los Angeles, CA—1 Mar 2015

Darrell Gatewood, Oklahoma City, OK
—1 Mar 2015

Deontre Dorsey, White Plains, MD
—1 Mar 2015

Thomas Allen Jr., Wellston, MO
— 28 Feb 2015

Calvon Reid, Coconut Creek, FL
—22 Feb 2015

Terry Price, Tulsa, OK—20 Feb 2015

Natasha McKenna, Fairfax, VA—8 Feb 2015

Jeremy Lett, Tallahassee, FL—4 Feb 2015

Alvin Haynes, San Bruno, CA—26 Jan 2015

Tiano Meton, Sierra Blanca, TX—22 Jan 2015

Andre Larone Murphy Sr., Norfolk, NE
—7 Jan 2015

Brian Pickett, Los Angeles, CA—6 Jan 2015

Leslie Sapp, Knoxville, PA—6 Jan 2015

Matthew Ajibade, Savannah, GA—1 Jan 2015

Rumain Brisbon, 34, Phoenix, Ariz.
—2 Dec 2014

Tamir Rice, 12, Cleveland, Ohio
—22 Nov 2014

Akai Gurley, 28, Brooklyn, NY—20 Nov 2014

Kajieme Powell, 25, St. Louis, MO
—19 Aug 2014

Ezell Ford, 25, Los Angeles, CA
—12 Aug 2014

Dante Parker, 36, San Bernardino County, CA
—12 Aug 2014

Michael Brown, 18, Ferguson, MO
—9 Aug 2014

John Crawford III, 22, Beavercreek, OH
—5 Aug 2014

Tyree Woodson, 38, Baltimore, MD
—2 Aug 2014

Eric Garner, 43, New York, NY—17 Jul 2014

Victor White III, 22, Iberia Parish, LA
—22 Mar 2014

Yvette Smith, 47, Bastrop, TX—16 Feb 2014

McKenzie Cochran, 25, Southfield, MI
—28 Jan 2014

Jordan Baker, 26, Houston, TX—16 Jan 2014

Andy Lopez, 13, Santa Rosa, CA
—22 Oct 2013

Miriam Carey, 34, Washington, DC
—3 Oct 2013

Jonathan Ferrell, 24, Bradfield Farms, NC
—14 Sept 2013

Carlos Alcis, 43, New York, NY
—15 Aug 2013

Larry Eugene Jackson, Jr., 32, Austin, TX
—26 Jul 2013

Deion Fludd, 17, New York, NY—5 May 2013

Kimani Gray, 16, New York, NY—9 Mar 2013

Malissa Williams, 30, Cleveland, OH
—29 Nov 2012

Timothy Russell, 43, Cleveland, OH
—29 Nov 2012

Reynaldo Cuevas, 20, New York, NY
—7 Sept 2012

Chavis Carter, 21, Jonesboro, AR
—29 Jul 2012

Shantel Davis, 23, New York, NY
—14 Jun 2012

Sharmel Edwards, 49, Las Vegas, NV
—21 Apr 2012

Tamon Robinson, 27, New York, NY
—18 Apr 2012

Ervin Jefferson, 18, Atlanta, GA
—24 Mar, 2012

Kendrec McDade, 19, Pasadena, CA
—24 Mar 2012

Rekia Boyd, 22, Chicago, IL—21 Mar 2012

Shereese Francis, 30, New York, NY
—15 Mar 2012

Wendell Allen, 20, New Orleans, LA
—7 Mar 2012

Nehemiah Dillard, 29, Gainesville, FL
—5 Mar 2012

Dante Price, 25, Dayton, OH—1 Mar 2012

Raymond Allen, 34, Galveston, TX
—27 Feb 2012

Sgt. Manuel Loggins, Jr., 31, Orange County, CA
—7 Feb 2012

Ramarley Graham, 18, New York, NY
—2 Feb 2012

Kenneth Chamberlain, 68, White Plains, NY
—19 Nov 2011

Alonzo Ashley, 29, Denver, CO—18 Jul 2011

Kenneth Harding, 19, San Francisco, CA
—16 Jul 2011

"This is flesh I'm talking about here. Flesh that needs to be loved. Feet that need to rest and to dance; backs that need support; shoulders that need arms, strong arms I'm telling you. And O my people, out yonder, hear me, they do not love your neck unnoosed and straight. So love your neck; put a hand on it, grace it, stroke it and hold it up. and all your inside parts that they'd just as soon slop for hogs, you got to love them. The dark, dark liver— love it, love it and the beating heart, love that too. More than eyes or feet. More than lungs that have yet to draw free air. More than your life-holding womb and your life-giving private parts, hear me now, love your heart. For this is the prize."
— Toni Morrison,
Beloved

Names compiled from http://gawker.com/unarmed-people-of-color-killed-by-police-1999-2014-1666672349; http://mappingpoliceviolence.org/unarmed/; and https://www.theguardian.com/us-news/ng-interactive/2015/jun/01/the-counted-police-killings-us-database.

CHAPTER NINE

Feelings about Heritage

Who will ever forget the moment of sheer #BlackGirlMagic when, in June 2015, Bree Newsome courageously climbed the thirty-foot flagpole on the grounds of the South Carolina state capitol building and took down the Confederate battle flag that had too long flown above it?

I won't. I wasn't even concerned about the Confederate battle flag. It's racist. Anyone who says differently is either lying to themselves or simply doesn't understand what racism is. However, of all the battles to be fought, it wasn't at the top of my list. Nonetheless, when notice of Bree's daring came across Twitter and I saw the video footage, my heart skipped a beat. Who was that fearless woman, scaling poles while quoting scripture? I was immediately a fan.

Bree didn't ask permission. Yes, she planned, and she collaborated, for sure. But she didn't talk the issue to death. She saw an injustice, and she did what she could about it— consequences be damned.

From what I've heard in her interviews, it wasn't an incapacitatingly complex matter for Bree. I think she understood the evil that had been done in that flag's name. I think more importantly, she knew the power of symbols and the stories they conveyed. I think she knew the traumatic impact those stories have on the lives of persons living under their brutal weight. I think she knew the physical, psychic, and material wounds we have suffered under the relentless lash of their repeated telling. They are wounds that have never been treated and allowed to heal.

Bree and her ten co-conspirators claimed healing for themselves. No more open, festering wound for

> Telling better stories benefits both the historically marginalized and the historically privileged.

them. And as my wife, Leslie, said to me, "When you heal, you heal your ancestors."

Everything Costs Something

That healing the present to heal the past . . . or following through in the present to commitments of the past . . . correcting in the present wrongs of the past, seems to be a part of even our oldest stories.

If you've ever heard the story of Moses, you may have gotten the idea that all the confusion in Moses's life happened before the burning bush, and that after the burning bush, everything was pretty straight forward: Moses goes home, tells his family what he has to do, packs his bags, goes to Egypt and gets the job done.[1] There may have been some struggle along the way—some things Moses had to contend with—but Moses is often depicted as a man crystal clear as to his purpose and mission. However, that was not the case, as Aaron likely learned a few nights after he met up with his brother's family at Mount Sinai while they journeyed toward Egypt (and Hollywood immortalization, i.e., whitewashing).

> "So what did Zipporah say when you told her?" Aaron inquired upon sharing his own story and hearing of his younger brother's remarkable encounter with God.
>
> "She was all for it—until she found out what it would cost."
>
> "What do you mean?"
>
> "After my father-in-law, Jethro, gave us his blessing, we spent the rest of the day preparing for the journey and left early the following morning. We kept a good pace. As desert dwellers, Zipporah's people know how to travel. By the end of the day, our son Geshom was very tired. We made camp and Zipporah laid the child down. As I stayed awake and prayed, the Lord spoke to me and said I must circumcise my son now, at the outset of our pilgrimage, as Abraham had done, as an act of faith and covenant.
>
> "The next morning I told Zipporah what the Lord asked of us. To my astonishment, she flatly refused. 'You will not cut my son! That is not a custom among my people.

[1] At least that's what The Prince of Egypt, Ridley Scott and Charlton Heston tried to teach me.

It may be something mothers among your people allow, but I will not. And if you try to do it anyway, I'll go back to my parents and leave you to return to Egypt by yourself.'

"I had no idea what to do. I just decided to drop it. I figured we could talk about it at another time. I saw no reason to force the issue; Zipporah had already left her family for me, something she could never have anticipated having to do. We were on our way to Egypt in response to the Lord's command. That was enough for the time being, or so I thought."

> "To act is to be committed, and to be committed is to be in danger."
> ~James Baldwin, author and social observer

"The next morning I woke up, and it felt like a boulder was lying on my chest. It felt as if God were trying to kill me. I couldn't breathe; I couldn't talk; I could barely move. I was scared to death. I was only able to reach out and swat at Zipporah. She awoke, startled by such a violent call into a new day. When she perceived how I moved and grabbed at my chest, she began to howl with fear. She kept asking, "What's wrong? What must I do?" She cried out to God on my behalf. Then in the midst of her prayer she ran out the tent.

"My eyes rolled around my head as I rolled around the floor of our tent, snatching momentary glances of the crimson ceiling and the purple blankets and the brown earth and the white light of day . . . and . . . and . . . I thought I glimpsed Zipporah returning, brandishing a flint knife. I became even more afraid now of what she might do to me!

"Instead she seemed to be moving toward Gershom. I thought she was losing her mind. I summoned all the strength within me. I rolled over to my hands and knees. The ground teetered beneath me as I struggled to rise to my feet. I gripped my chest even tighter and dropped to one knee, using my free hand to break my fall. I groped toward her but toppled over. I watched in initial horror as my wife tore the clothes from my sleeping son's body, takes something out of her mouth that she's been chewing, applies whatever it was liberally to the boy's midsection, waits a moment and then proceeds to quickly peel the foreskin from his penis with the knife. Once done, she immediately applied a salve to

Geshom's wounded pride. I don't know which hurt more at that moment, my chest or the sight of my son being circumcised unexpectedly.

"Zipporah then does the weirdest thing. She slings the boy's foreskin at me. It lands and clings to the big toe of my right foot, and she screams at the top of her lungs something like, "You bloody husband!" After that, she turns, runs and falls into an embrace of Gershom who by now is writhing in discomfort on his sleeping mat.

"The surprising detail of this observation slowly brought two awarenesses to my attention. First, that my chest was no longer hurting. Second, that despite my gratitude for the first awareness, I was far from pain free. Perhaps in sympathy for my son or perhaps because my wife snuck a kick in, my loins were throbbing!

"Wow. That's some stuff," replied a stunned Aaron. "All that over brit milah (circumcision). Who would have thought that circumcision was important enough to almost lose your life over?"

"I don't know, but I've been trying to make sense of it all. Perhaps its importance reflects the seriousness of undeterred devotion. I've been thinking about everything that has happened in my life," Moses reminisced. "Early on, I was in such a hurry to complete the story of being a deliverer to my people. Now, once I've finally given up on my ability to affect any change for the Hebrews and so many Hebrews have given up believing a change is going to come, here comes God saying the time has come.

"I was first tempted to think that everything I experienced and learned in my youth was worthless—whether it was the stories our mother, Jochebed, told me as my nurse or the ceremonies, feasts, and social responsibilities I learned to celebrate while with you, even our own circumcisions. You know I, like so many of our kin, have completely forsaken or forgotten the old ways. I had even labeled hollow the scholarly, political, and cultural lessons I learned in Pharaoh's court. It had all begun to seem pretty useless to me as I wandered the desert with Jethro's sheep. But maybe it wasn't. Maybe my timing was off, but the devotion was no less important. And in order to complete this task, I have to go back and reclaim some things, correct some things and create some new things to move forward."

"Well, like the elders say," Aaron chimed in, "'Everything costs something—good or bad.' Either you pay the cost in devotion to the task you are about to undertake, or you pay the cost of not following through.

"And one doesn't get to choose the terms of the responsibility or the consequence for remaining irresponsible either," Moses concurred as he used a stick to poke the fire that warmed their late night conversation. "Each task requires what it requires."

Aaron yawned and stretched, ready for bed. After a poignant pause, he asked, "So how's Geshom feeling after his ordeal?"

"Well, let's just say he was relieved when the day's walk had ended."

"Yeah, there's just no comfortable travel in his condition." They both chuckled uneasily at the thought.

"The upside is that the trip can only get better from here on out."

"Sure. Provided we don't wander into any plagues along the way."

"But what are the odds of that happening?"

"You're an eighty-year-old fugitive who was told by fiery vegetation to demand that the most powerful ruler in this part of the world let all his free labor just leave, and your only credibility is a staff that turns into a snake and a spokesman who is enslaved himself."

"Well when you put it that way, it does sound a bit absurd, but stranger things have happened."

"Oh, yeah, when?"

In All Sincerity

The intuition that arises for me out of this story is that we honor the past by improving upon it. That intuition brings me full circle with the need for COMPOSTable stories. Each generation has to

> We honor the past by improving upon it.

find its own commitment to the stories and rituals of their faith, just like Moses himself, which starts with **C**onfession and holding **O**pposing forces in tension and **M**eekness and **P**osing questions and **O**thers-interestedness and **S**usceptibility to harm and treating **T**radition as a living word. At the end of the day, the goal of the COMPOST matrix is to provide a simple framework by which to understand how better stories work and to offer you a method by which to engage in the same practice. There is nothing sacred about the framework itself. What is sacred are the stories that inspire us to "the better angels of our nature."[2]

This intuition of honoring the past by improving upon it recurs, at least implicitly, in scripture. I first encountered it telling the story of Gideon during my final talk at the Wild Goose Festival in 2014.[3] I had just finished delineating the differences between what I called "The Feast of What Is Becoming" versus "The Leftovers of What Has Been," and we had moved into a question-response period. A middle-aged Southern white woman raised her hand and, with tears streaming down her face, proceeded to ask me about the moral dilemma she was having reconciling the truth of her Southern slave-owning, lynching, Jim Crow-embodying, segregationist, racist, discriminatory heritage and the family members who have and still emulate this way, but whom she loves, with the person she wants to be in the world. I was reminded of a Midwestern Hebrew Israelite black man who once told me of growing up without his parents, who spent most of his childhood in prison on repeated drug convictions. Even though his parents weren't in his life when and how he needed them as a child, he spends every day of his adult life trying to honor his father and mother like the Good Book says. "It doesn't say, 'Honor them *only if* they were good parents,'" he said to me with a smirk, "It simply says honor them."

I shared that story with the tearful woman, adding, "We don't honor our fathers and mothers by making all the same mistakes they made. We honor them by doing better." What struck me was the weight I saw fall from the woman's shoulders. I had by no means given her an easy way out. There was plenty of hard work to be done to right the wrongs she knew her family was guilty of or complicit in. But she had found a path forward. That encounter confirmed for me the value in telling better stories for both the historically marginalized and the historically privileged.

[2] A turn of phrase by Abraham Lincoln in his first Inaugural Address.

[3] "Losing Our Appetite for Beloved Community." http://melvinbray.com/2014/07/08/losing-our-appetite-for-beloved-community/.

[4] The one Christian story that perfectly captures the devotion of which I speak is the story of Jesus, a Messiah unwilling to be satisfied with self-sacrificial death on the cross—the part that so many of us praise and admire. However, the hard part, the part that took faith and devotion, was the comeback, the Resurrection, the divine challenge to all humanity to respond better the second time around to a Creator's indomitable belief in the goodness of all creation. For more on a theology oriented this way, check out Danielle Shroyer's *Original Blessing* (Minneapolis: Fortress, 2016).

The difficulty in communicating the type of dedication, determination, and follow-through needed to live this intuition is that we lack strong English words for the kind of commitment I'm trying to express. We are so used to substituting words for actions. Neither "dedication" nor "determination" is broad enough to encompass the concept of honoring the past by improving upon it from beginning to end. "Commitment" is almost too broad, too many alternate definitions that distract from the point. "Devotion" is perhaps the most accurate, but it's a Muslim or Jewish type of devotion—even a nonreligious devotion—as opposed to the Christian "I read my devotional reading for the day" type of devotion[4]. "Follow-through" gets to the most vital part, but it implies little about how one must start or even prepare. Devoting one's self to honoring the past by improving upon it means to follow-through to better, even in the face of the criticism of those who claim to be on the side of justice, but because of timidity, misplaced loyalty or lack of true conviction, would rather slow walk the future into being. To them we say no.

> "People can cry much easier than they can change."
> ~James Baldwin, author and social observer

The World that Is Becoming

To call me a political junkie would be an understatement. I watched MHP (Melissa Harris-Perry) religiously before it went off the air (#NerdlandForever!),[5] listen to NPR, and read several online news outlets on a regular basis. In an election year that consumption tends to increase exponentially. Most of my online writing revolves around it.[6] I'm thoroughly intrigued by politics, particularly its intersection with social justice.

My political itch has most recently been scratched by the bestseller *Brown Is the New White*[7], by Steve Phillips, a political operative and former politician. Through extensive in-depth research, Phillips has identified a voting block of consistently progressive voters, which he calls "the New American Majority." As of 2012, they made up "51 percent of the country's citizen voting age population, and that majority is getting bigger every single day." So when a newly elected President Barack Obama said in his first inaugural address, "What the cynics fail to understand is that *the ground has shifted beneath them,* that the stale political arguments that have consumed us for so long no longer apply," he knew of what he spoke.[8]

[5] Thank God for Democracy Now!

[6] Of all the writing I've ever done, the highlight of my career so far was the opportunity to respond for Sojo.net to then Candidate Barack Obama's so-called "race speech" delivered in Philadelphia, PA, at Constitution Hall in 2008. I actually got in advance what they call an "embargoed copy" of the speech, so that I could have my response already written for publication the moment he said, "And may God bless these United States."

[7] Steve Phillips, *Brown Is the New White* (New York: New Press, 2016).

[8] Sadly, this has recently come up for debate within the Democratic party both after and during the 2016 US presidential election, which I believe helps to explain why they lost. Their loss of focus—lack of devotion to this new reality—left me shaking my head.

Here is a brief overview of the numbers. Sixty percent of white voters have consistently voted conservative over the past forty-five years; forty percent have consistently voted progressive. Those numbers fluctuate very little. People of color, on the other hand, overwhelmingly vote for social justice, which is to say they vote progressive, but—and here's the catch—they don't vote with the same frequency.[9] The reason the New American Majority is getting bigger with each passing day is because of the dramatic difference between birth and death rates among Americans of color and white Americans, plus the influx of immigrants. Up from the 2012 totals, the New American Majority is composed of nearly half people of color. Obama won two terms because this New American Majority showed up at the polls in 2008 and in 2012 in record numbers. Progressive candidates lost in 2010 and 2014 because a substantial number of eligible voters of color stayed home or weren't registered both times. The primary thing progressives have to do to win any election going forward is to build platforms that excite people of color by speaking to that which concerns them. It's that simple.

One of the most compelling implications of this New American Majority is that its mere existence will no longer allow America to subsist on "the leftovers of What Has Been." No more business as usual. And to the degree that this coalition really chooses to exercise its political muscle, it can literally reshape the face and function of politics in America.

One of the key areas in which Steve Phillips advocates for the reshaping of America to happen is in comprehensive immigration *transformation*.[10] I echo this hope. The idea that, as a country of immigrants who overran the indigenous population without reparations, we would now complain about being overrun by immigrants whose home economies, governments, and ways of life we helped to devastate is hypocrisy I can't abide. Phillips offers more detail:

> Progressives are often too apologetic when it comes to advocating for immigration reform, frequently accepting the narrative that many people are here 'illegally.' . . . America has a long and explicitly racist history on this issue. Between stealing land from the Native Americans (making the early English settlers and America's founders the original illegal immigrants), codifying racism into the 'free White persons' restriction of the first naturalization

[9] This is due to a lot of reasons, including active voter suppression on the part of political conservatives, inadequate voter registration, mobilization, and anti-suppression work on the part of political liberals, and ongoing alienation from either major party.

[10] My word, not his. After chapter 8, I can't use the word "reform."

law, passing the Chinese Exclusion Act, and establishing a racially restrictive national immigration quota system in the 1920s that continues to influence the modern policy debate, conservatives are the ones who should be apologizing.

An effective and pro-active approach to immigration reform should encompass at least four core components. First, yes, provide amnesty to everyone who is here and undocumented. . . . We should especially expedite the process to keep families together. More than 4 million people have applied to be reunited with their families, and humanity, compassion, and family values should dictate immediate—and favourable—action on these applications. Second, progressives need to make large-scale naturalization of the 9 million undocumented immigrants who can become citizens quickly a top priority. This will expand the constituency of those who understand the Immigrant experience. . . . After addressing those who are here, reforms should focus on the issue of future immigration. . . . First, we need to reconfigure the current system for allocation of visas…. Ultimately, we need to step back and look at the root causes of why people are coming here in the first place.[11]

Steve Phillips is right, but neither major political party is paying attention. Both are obsessing over the mirage of "the white working class [swing] voter."[12] The progressive establishment may have to lose big a few times before it registers. Meanwhile, those devoted to better, some at great risk to themselves,[13] stand in solidarity with Dreamers, the Sanctuary Movement and anyone else lifting a voice in this fight to acknowledge the basic human dignities of immigrants. We are in the streets demonstrating. We are taking families in need of sanctuary into our homes and churches. We are lobbying legislators. We are disrupting deportations with our very bodies. We are researching and crafting theologies, policies and persuasive messaging. We are educating those ignorant to the injustice. We are raising money. We are giving money. We are coordinating and collaborating and strategizing the next campaigns, initiatives and actions. We are helping people get their footing in this country when they are allowed to settle. We are defending them from harassment. We are doing what we can to honor our deeply problematic immigration past by improving upon it. And more, so much more,

[11] Ibid.

[12] Remember how neatly white votes divide between conservative and progressive. There is simply no such pool from which to siphon votes.

[13] Check out *Out of the Closet, Out of the Shadows*, filmmaker Robert Winn, to learn about LGBTQIA leadership in the struggle against deportation. Available at https://vimeo.com/145664693.

> "When you heal, you heal your ancestors."
> ~Leslie Bray, community organizer

[14] This need for devotion is true of any number of social challenges. Michelle Alexander discusses it in relationship to dismantling the prison industrial complex in her seminal *The New Jim Crow* (New York: New Press, 2010, 2012), "If we hope to end the system of control, we cannot be satisfied with a handful of reforms. All of the financial incentives granted to law enforcement to arrest poor black and brown people for drug offenses must be revoked. Federal grant money for drug enforcement must end; drug forfeiture laws must be stripped from the books; racial profiling must be eradicated; the concentration of drug busts in poor communities of color must cease; and the transfer of military equipment and aid to local law enforcement agencies waging the drug war must come to a screeching halt. And that's just for starters."

[15] Or as Obama remixed it, "Yes we can!"

still needs to be done until *outcomes* change—not feelings, not intentions, not words—outcomes![14]

When ordinary words failed, our forebears reached for metaphor, ritual, and song (the stuff of story) to articulate and inspire their undying devotion to better—a devotion born out of the sweat of oppression. In the fields they sang, "I opened my mouth to the Lord, and I won't turn back; I will go, I shall go, to see what the end is going to be." As they marched they sang, "Ain't gonna let nobody turn me round, turn me round, turn me round. Ain't gonna let nobody turn me round. Keep on walkin', keep on talkin', marchin' up to freedom's land." And when there was far too much to put into song, they simply said, "Sí, se puede!"[15]

CHAPTER TEN

Better World

I grew up in a church more diverse than most. Our church was about 50 percent white, 30 percent black, 15 percent Asian, and 5 percent Latino. From a kid's point of view, it was a wonderful place. It felt close-knit. On any given weekend a gang of families would gather at someone's home and hang out all day and into the night. We laughed a lot. We went on day trips together. We kids went to school together, at least early on. We did scouting-type stuff together.[1] I made lifelong friendships with folks who are really more like family.

[1] Instead of the Scouts, we were the Pathfinders.

The church definitely had its problems. It never quite got power dynamics right, particularly after we lost our Pacific Islander pastor. The school the church ran eventually shut down because of it. We suffered a succession of mass exits of congregants because of it. However, as a little kid, I didn't know all that. As far as I knew, my church was what society looked like. It was my normal.

My spouse and I have made a conscious decision to limit the amount of religion we pass on to our children.

Of course, I soon discovered how rare it was for people to even try to connect across differences, and the challenges they face when they do. After a stint in predominantly white elementary and middle schools, I went to a historically black high school and college, taught at a predominantly black high school and went to a predominantly black church for several years. I love my people. However, I kept being seduced into these various interracial, ecumenical, multi-faith or open-and-affirming spaces as well. As one who transgresses boundaries fairly easily, I love that too, and I have put in a lot of work to help such spaces thrive. It wasn't until I hit forty that I realized I'd spent my adult life chasing an image of beloved community that resembled the church of my upbringing.

[2] Despite what we see on television in western society, the world is plenty diverse.

[3] If you have kids younger than nine, do yourself a favor and pick it up: *Free to Be You & Me* by Marlo Thomas.

[4] Israel, circa 970 to 931 BCE.

[5] Ecclesiastes 4:12

Whereas I don't believe that diversity alone makes the world better,[2] I do think this impulse to seek a world where we all are "free to be you and me"[3] is important. For one thing, the impulse itself affirms all is not right when one doesn't feel that freedom. For another, it assures us we are not alone in wanting and, hopefully, doing the work to achieve better. The better I imagine possible can't be achieved individually. Yes, it is about each of us finding better ways of showing up in the world, but the purpose of that showing up is to relate better with one another. The biggest most complex problems in the world—racism, sexism, heterosexism, ableism, religious hatred, ecological disregard—are relational, not individual, and they have solutions that can only be achieved relationally. My goal in writing this book has been to inspire readers, particularly those inhibited by hostile faith stories, to join those of us already collaborating to make a more beautiful, more just, more virtue-filled world.

In Case You Missed It

A wise African king named Solomon[4] is remembered saying something like, "A three-strand cord is not easily broken."[5] Throughout this book I've done three things repeatedly: (1) tell a story; (2) share the intuition that arises out of it for me; and (3) identify what part of the COMPOST method was at work in my telling of the story. By doing these three things, I've sought to weave three distinct ideas, each worthy of its own book; but together I believe they make a nearly unbreakable case that better is possible. All three are bound together in my exercise of the COMPOST method as fully articulated in chapter 1, so as to encourage by example your own practice of better storytelling. Let's review each idea strand individually. For once, I will be as linear in my explanation as possible.

Strand 1: The Significance of Story

I've been trying to convince you of the significance of story, not just its historic significance, but its present impact on our daily lives. Rather than reason through logic, I wanted to entice you with how it makes you feel when you encounter a life-giving story. Better story fires the imagination. Better story births possibilities you didn't know you had. Better story emboldens you with something toward which to aspire.

People without story are without direction. That's why with all the many different formats from which to choose, historian Vincent

Harding chose to write the story of the struggle of people stolen from Africa in the Trans-Atlantic Slave Trade as a narrative history. His book, *There is a River*[6], is the story of our struggle for liberation and justice, not our enslavement. This desire for direction is why Alex Haley wrote *Roots*. It's the reason Toni Morrison wrote *Beloved* and *The Bluest Eye,* and Alice Walker wrote *The Color Purple* and *Meridian* . . . Lorraine Hansberry staged *A Raisin in the Sun* and August Wilson staged *The Piano Lesson* . . . Spike Lee made *Malcolm X* and Ava Duvernay made *Selma*.[7] We are not a people without story.

Again, I'm not talking about just any story. I'm talking about the stories around which we organize both our individual thoughts, attitudes, and actions and our societal/cultural norms, mores, and philosophies. They become our cultural touchstones for figuring new things out, our common frames of reference for judging validity, our social landmarks for locating ourselves in relationship to others. Literature professors call them myths to differentiate them from stories of the garden variety. They are stories that have the power to change the way we see the world, which is exactly what each of the stories in the previous paragraph did for me.

> Faith stories have the power to change the way we see and choose to be in the world.

To understand how powerful even simple myths are, take for example the myth that "Animals are people too" popularized by half the Disney cartoons on the market. This notion has spawned a billion-dollar commercial industry around elective animal care. Never mind the fact that animals have thrived on this planet for hundreds of thousands of years without human provision and most still do. Somehow, some way, Westerners have gotten it in our heads that dutiful dog owners pay to have their pets shorn, then buy them sweaters to keep them warm in the cold. God forbid what we would do to cats if they would abide it. In addition to the toys and trinkets especially designed for one's specific species and breed, the doting owner—I mean companion—can now invest in the services of specialists who specialize in animal parties, animal massage,[8] and animal psycho-therapy to help our anthropomorphic pals feel good about themselves, their work, and the passing years.

But it's not just the stuff we do to preen and pamper our pets. Animal health care has us conflicted as well. I was in the supermarket the other day and a fellow shopper was in

[6] Vincent Harding, *There is a River: the Black Stuggle for Freedom in America* (New York: Mariner Books, 1993)

[7] Of course, I feel tempted to name every story on my bookshelf.

[8] My wife, a certified massage therapist, is seriously considering breaking into this specialty.

one breath telling me where I could find the cheapest dog food, while at the same time extolling the virtues of the most expensive animal victuals on the market. Have you ever seen a dog actually out being a dog? Dogs will eat anything. Even their own poop. And boy, do they love to roll in it. Given the option to drink clean, clear water versus the muddy or greening water of an algae- infested pond, dogs will opt for the colored water as often as not.[9] Nonetheless, there are so many ailments from which one can have one's furry or feathered friend vaccinated and so many new ways to stave off the inevitable that the circle of life is now an ellipse. The cost of all this animal care is such that insurance companies have gotten in on the action. From goldfish open heart surgery to feline AIDS treatment, animal health care is big business.

Meanwhile, it's not like the United States leads the world in our ethical treatment of animals. Our industrial meat systems may be state-of-the-art but are far from humane.[10] Not only do we consume more meat than any other nation except China,[11] we hunt for sport. I don't know for sure, but I'm willing to bet that most of those buying beak warmers for their birds aren't lifelong members of PETA.[12]

Don't get me wrong, if you have an extra $5,000 to give an animal reconstructive surgery after it's been maimed, by all means, have at it. It just seems to me that might come after eradicating the problems of food insecurity and homelessness in one's neighborhood and the one next door. The fact that we haven't eradicated human hunger in my country, a nation that spends as much as we do in provision for our pets, leaves me with some concerns about our intuitions of justice and compassion. It used to be that if an animal found himself hurt beyond all usefulness, whoever had the stomach would take the wretched creature out back and put him out of his misery. Nowadays that would land one in jail. The fact that many can watch dogs and cats being rescued in the aftermath of Katrina and even now be moved to tears, yet feel ambivalent about the uses of language of "refugees" and "looters" to describe the people trying to survive there, who had not been rescued and had lost all provision is disturbing.[13] But that's the power of myth at work in our lives.

Faith stories, what we might otherwise call "sacred myths," have this same kind of significance.

---

[9] Kids will often try this at least once too.

[10] See the 2008 documentary *Food, Inc.,* director Robert Kenner.

[11] Which has a billion people compared to the USA's 300 million. "Meat Consumption by Type and Country," International Statistics, The 2012 Statistical Abstract, US Census Bureau (census.gov).

[12] Mind you, I eat meat, and I own a shotgun. I'm not against the purposeful utilization of animals and animal products to support human life, but it seems to me that leading the world in both consumption of animals that outstrips physical need and a sentimentality related to animals that's beyond all use speaks of a worldview at odds with itself.

[13] Just as disturbing as Michigan Gov. Rick Snyder overseeing the poisoning of an entire city of people (Flint), which will have health and socioeconomic repercussions for generations to come, just to save a few pennies.

Strand 2: The Right to Reimagine

The downside of being raised in the fundamentalist church environment I described at the beginning of the chapter was that, although a lot of conversation was had about the love of God, a lot of the stories focused on the wrath of God. Oddly, that was called love too. I can't overstate how this warps one's understanding of love. In our stories God got away with stuff we would call abusive in any other relationship and somehow could still claim to love us.

What that meant is that we grew up with a kind of schizophrenic notion of God and who we are meant to be in relationship to God. "If God isn't someone to be feared," a college friend of mine recently noted, "we don't trust him." As wee children, our parents taught us songs like, "Be careful, little hands, what you do . . . For the Father up above is looking down in love. So be careful little hands what you do. Be careful, little eyes, what you see . . . little ears what you hear . . . little feet where you go . . . little mouths what you say . . . ." Few ever questioned, "If God is looking down in love, what do I have to be careful about?" If they did, the verbal answer was, "Disappointing him." But, of course, the real answer was, "Going to hell."

Examples of this line of religious indoctrination through story and ritual are endless. They lodge within one's consciousness and affect the way we see the world and our place in it. Some of us escape the torment by walking away from these stories completely. Far more remain schizophrenic in order to stay committed to the stories, and it shows up in occasionally hostile and inconsistent ways. I'm proposing a third way. What if we just reimagine the stories to match the virtues they are meant to extoll? Simply by doing it over and over for eight chapters, I'm trying to demonstrate our right to do it.

Never mind the fact that this is what human beings have always done, even within the Christian tradition. Take just one example that crosses multiple religious traditions: the beautiful imagery of the virgin birth. This was the story that restored within the Christian tradition, which in its Jewish roots had been so male dominated, an appreciation of the feminine as the source of life and sustenance.[14] But as hard as it is for some to hear, the image of the Madonna is not unique to Christianity; Christianity wasn't even the first to use it. In ancient Egypt, we first encounter the

[14] In my best David Alan Grier impression, "Wrote a story about it. Want to read it? Here it go!" It's on my blog: http://findourselves.blogspot.com/2015/12/occupy-bethlehem.html.

story cast in stone and painted on temple walls: Isis suckling her son Horus whose conception was shrouded in the mystery of his father, Osiris, being dead at the time he impregnated Isis. Not to be outdone, the Greeks remix the story to have Zeus planting his seed all over the place in the form of swans, serpents, and husbands. In Greek mythology, Leda, Persephone, Alcmene (and many others) are all women who experience what Christians have coined an "immaculate conception" (i.e., a baby minus the sex). Getting in on the action, Hindus embedded the concept of the birth-of-the-divine-out-of-the-human in learning of the centers of spiritual power in the human body, known as the chakras; the fourth chakra represents the birth of compassion, the Hindu and Buddhist correlation to the Jesus message. So it is not surprising that in Buddhism, this motif is repeated, combined again with mother-child imagery, for the Buddha is said to have been born out of his mother's side at a point parallel to the heart, the location of the fourth chakra.[15] All of these uses of virgin birth imagery to tell one's faith story predate Christianity. This should not be seen as discrediting the Christian story; but rather, affirming to all uses of the Madonna image that they must be hitting on something important in humanity's pursuit of better. Otherwise, it wouldn't be such a common motif.[16]

Most people groups have understood the need for a living set of stories and rituals that evolve and trade up for images more beautiful, more just, and more virtue-filled. It's only within Western society that we somehow got the idea that instead of living rituals (stories enacted) we could have inanimate institutions that would keep everything the same forever.[17]

Our stories not only have the right to change over time, I hope it has become abundantly clear as you've encounter the stories herein that they need to change. Alex Haley hints at this in the first four chapters of *Roots*, during the time that Kunta Kinte is still safe in his village, coming of age and learning the stories of his people from "beloved, mysterious and peculiar old Nyo Boto," one of the village grandmothers. Haley writes, "No matter how bad anything was, Nyo Boto would always remember a time when it was worse."[18] Which is to say, my incredibly insightful spouse suggested, "Her stories evolved to meet the needs of her village, to encourage them that no matter what they were going through, they could make it."

[15] These connections are made by mythologist Joseph Campbell in his acclaimed PBS interview with Bill Moyer, *The Power of Myth.*

[16] I wish I could be as inclusive as this on every point demonstrating the connections between all our mythologies, but that's a different book: to be written by an ensemble of faith practitioners from various traditions and not just one Westerner who has appointed himself the neutral arbiter of everyone else's stories. I was raised in the Christian tradition, its stories are the ones in which I find myself, so herein I speak primarily of Judeo-Christian stories because they are my stories, respecting others' right to do the same with their own stories.

[17] This is a much deeper realization than my need to focus will allow me to unpack. Check out Malidoma Patrice Somé's book *Ritual: Power, Healing, and Community* and that of his spouse, Sombonfu Somé, *The Spirit of Intimacy.*

[18] Alex Haley, *Roots* (Garden City, NY: Doubleday, 1976), 10–11.

Everyone has the right to make it through. I just happen to be done with faith stories in which making it through means barely surviving. We deserve better.

Strand 3: The Ends Matter

I have chosen as my desired end the practice of beloved community. It is to that end that I tell the faith stories I tell. As you've read, I hope you've gotten the distinct impression that by "faith," I mean something far better than "religion," which for me has been a rather unsavory mix of self-interests that often subvert the COMPOST impulses in faith. Faith, on the other hand, is a cosmic intuition that better is possible, if we would but dare to seek it.

Leslie and I have made a conscious decision to limit the amount of religion we pass on to our children. We grew up steeped in church. Our children are not. Religion is typically the means through which parents teach faith. So without immersion in religion, we've had to be quite intentional about pointing them toward ends that matter.

We do have faith practices. We gather in faith with a community of friends who remind one another of the hopes we share that a better world is possible. We practice with each other what we hope are better ways of being in the world now, and we direct those energies outward in hopes of joining God in making all things new. However, over the years we've noticed that, whenever it came time to speak to our

> "Children have never been very good at listening to their elders, but they have never failed to imitate them."
> ~James Baldwin, author and social observer

children about the better intuitions we've found in our faith, there was always a tendency to reach for the particular stories and rituals with which we grew up. It's infuriating, because these are the same stories and rituals—ways of seeing and being in the world—that nearly cost us our faith and that are currently costing so many others theirs. Despite our detours, our goal has been to cultivate for our kids a faith that is dynamic and rich with stories with a concept of better that seeks the good of others and not just themselves—i.e., beloved community.

In contrast, plenty of good-hearted people of faith think the end lies in the need to escape this planet before it quite literally bursts into flames. Their goal is to make their "calling and election sure" so that they end up in the air-conditioned seats for the

[19] Nosebleed section no matter!

main event.[19] That sense of the end is bound to produce a very different set of stories than those my faith community tells.

I'm not too concerned about the sweet by-and-by. According to the stories told to me in childhood, there's not a whole lot I can do about the afterlife anyhow. But I am concerned about the here-and-now. I know it can be better on many fronts, and if the stories that have been handed down to me are correct, I get to join God in making the here-and-now as beautiful, as just, and as virtue-filled as it can be. I'm all for that.

As I expressed in chapter 1, beloved community isn't about feeling good toward each other; it's about doing well in relationship to each other. That means beloved community is a political reality, but that is not to say it isn't also a deeply personal reality. As Lisa Sharon Harper, author of *The Very Good Gospel,* is apt to say, black and brown people's entire lives in the United States and other westernized spaces are intensely political. Where we live and how we move and who we marry—the most intimate details of our lives—are determined by the political realities of the spaces we inhabit. That is why most of the better intuitions explored herein have had unmistakably political applications to them. A better that doesn't reimagine the systems and structures of the world as it simultaneously evolves us personally isn't a better worth writing about.

> "Forget the lesser evil . . . fight for the greater good."
> ~Jill Stein, physician and advocate

[20] Martin Luther King Jr., "Where Do We Go From Here?" August 1967 speech to the Southern Christian Leadership Conference in Atlanta, Georgia.

Bend the Arc

Dr. King is often remembered for noting, "The arc of the moral universe is long, but it bends toward justice."[20] The challenge is that people of goodwill often act as if the arc of the moral universe bends toward justice on its own. It does not. God made humanity the catalyst toward this moral end. Unless people of goodwill act in good faith toward a just end, justice will not be found. Justice, like all other virtues, is a relational challenge seeking a relational response.

Recognize the tremendous hope in this realization. The sooner we get about the business of relating more justly, the sooner justice can be found. We participate with God in making all things new.

So if you go back and look at the expository arc of this book illustrated in the introduction, with the arc of which Martin Luther King Jr. spoke in mind, something should jump out at you visually. The practices of beloved community advocated herein are actions that bend the arc. So if you are serious about being a part of the justice that is becoming, you have to get serious about more beautiful, more just, more virtue-filled ways of being in the world. And if you want the "better" in those ways to live beyond you, then you have to let them infect the stories you pass on.

Better is possible. It doesn't take geniuses or experts. It doesn't matter if you're starting from a place of faith or of doubt.[21] We can just decide and move forward together. Whether you want to be a better person of faith, a better parent, a better storyteller, a better justice-seeker, a better writer, a better student, or a better entrepreneur . . . BETTER begins now.[22]

[21] You owe it to yourself to listen to Casey Gerald's "The Gospel of Doubt" (TED Talk) https://www.ted.com/talks/casey_gerald_the_gospel_of_doubt?language=en.

[22] Now go and treat yourself to a glass of ear intoxication with Lalah Hathaway and Joe Sample's "Come Along with Me." More BETTER playlist favorites can be found on the *BETTER* website better.melvinbray.com.